360° Success: The No-Regret Playbook for Entrepreneurs

By: Linh Podetti

360° Success: The No-Regret Playbook for Entrepreneurs

Published by: Linh Podetti

ISBN-13: 978-1-7637798-4-6

Printed in Australia

Disclaimer

This publication is designed to provide general information and inspiration for entrepreneurs. It is not intended to provide financial, legal, or medical advice. Readers should consult qualified professionals for advice tailored to their individual circumstances.

The author and publisher disclaim any liability, loss, or risk incurred as a consequence, directly or indirectly, of the use and application of any contents of this book. In developing this book, the author has drawn on research, personal experience, and the support of AI tools.

360° Success:

The No-Regret Playbook for Entrepreneurs

By: Linh Podetti

TABLE OF CONTENTS

Introduction

Welcome to 360° Success: The No-Regret Playbook for Entrepreneurs. If you're here, you're probably an entrepreneur who's achieved a level of success, but you're wondering... is this it?

Maybe your calendar is full but your heart isn't. Maybe your bank account's growing, but your peace of mind isn't. This book is your permission and your plan to make sure you don't look back with regret.

No regret over missed family time.
No regret over health neglected.
No regret over chasing success at the cost of your soul.

Because what's the point of building a business if it costs you your joy, your energy, or your purpose? 360° Success is about redefining what it means to "make it."

It's not just about revenue or titles. It's about designing a life you're proud of, where you're winning in business and in the things that matter most: your health, your family, your happiness, your peace. You'll find tools here to help you:

- Build a business that supports your lifestyle, not steals from it
- Design your life with intention
- Get clear on what truly matters to you
- Let go of the "shoulds" and lean into what's right for your season of life

This isn't theory. It's a playbook: practical and actionable.

What to Expect from This Book

As a fellow entrepreneur, I value systems, practical steps, and no-fluff advice. That's exactly what you'll find in this book.

At the end of each chapter, you'll get hands-on exercises, reflection tools, and strategic prompts to help you take real steps forward.

How to Use This Book:

- **Take It Slow:** Read one chapter at a time. Let it sink in. This isn't a race; it's a reset.
- **Reflect Honestly:** Your clarity starts with honesty. Be real with yourself.
- **Act Immediately:** Don't wait for the "perfect time." Small changes now prevent big regrets later.
- **Revisit Often:** These pages are here for every season. What you don't need today might save you tomorrow.

A Final Note Before We Begin

Before we dive into Chapter One, I want to share a little bit of my story of how I went from feeling overwhelmed and stretched thin as a business owner to becoming a fulfilled entrepreneur who lives with intention, freedom, and joy.

Today, I run a business that gives me the flexibility to travel the world, be present with my family, and work when and where I choose.

People often ask me, *"How are you living your best life?"* Or *"What's your secret?"*

That's exactly why I wrote this book: to share the mindset shift and system that changed my life, so you can use it to change yours too. Because if I can do it, so can you.

Understanding where I started might help you reflect on where you are now and more importantly, where you want to go next.

Let's turn the page and begin this journey together.

About The Author

Hey there! I'm Linh Podetti, founder of Outsourcing Angel, mum of three, global traveller, and entrepreneur of nearly 15 years.

I run a remote team of over 100 and have built multiple businesses from home... But it hasn't always been smooth sailing.

I was born in Vietnam and migrated to Australia at the age of nine. Life as a migrant wasn't easy. We were poor, and like many immigrant families, we did whatever it took to survive.

I became a child labourer from the age of ten, helping my parents with their home-based sewing business instead of just being a kid.

I struggled to fit in. I rebelled. I ran away. For a while, I felt completely lost. Caught in the wrong crowd, making the wrong choices, trying to find where I belonged.

Those early years shaped everything. I embrace a life of freedom now because I know exactly what it's like to grow up without it. My parents were strict and rarely let me go out.

The only "holidays" we had were visits back to Vietnam. I saw first-hand what self-employment looked like: No time. No fun. No connection with your kids. They worked around the clock, and although it was out of love and sacrifice, I grew up craving for their attention and love.

Then, at twenty, I became a single mum. That was the moment everything shifted.

Suddenly, life wasn't just about me anymore. I had someone depending on me. I knew I had to change the trajectory of my life for my son's future.

So I went back to university, got my degree, and found a "proper" job in the corporate world.

But it didn't take long to realise that the 9-to-5 grind wasn't built for mums like me. I had no flexibility, constant mum guilt, and zero time freedom. I felt like I was always choosing between career and family, and losing on both fronts.

That's when I took a leap and started my first business at the age of twenty-seven. I was chasing flexibility... But what I found was hardship. Business was hard. I started many businesses that failed. I wore every hat, worked around the clock, and barely made progress. But one decision changed everything. I discovered outsourcing.

While running an e-commerce store selling nail polish, I hired my first offshore team member. It was like a light bulb went off. For the first time, I felt the weight lift.

That one hire showed me a whole new way of building a business that didn't rely on me doing it all. From that moment, my direction shifted. I moved into marketing and virtual teams, eventually founding Outsourcing Angel. It's a company that helps entrepreneurs grow by building freedom-focused virtual teams. We match skilled freelancers, especially from the Philippines, with businesses in Australia, the US, and beyond. It's deeply rewarding.

Not just because we help businesses grow, but because we also create real job opportunities for people who deserve a better life. But even with all this freedom, I started to notice something troubling.

While I was helping entrepreneurs outsource to free up time, most weren't actually using that time to live better. They were just filling it with more work. And life?... It kept waiting.

That was the story of my own husband.

He runs a manufacturing company.

A traditional, hands-on operation that's consumed his time and energy for over twenty-five years. For years, I believed him when he said, *"Once I hire the right person..."* Or *"Once we move into the new factory, I'll finally have more time to spend it with the family."* But that time never came.

And he's not the only one.

I realised how many entrepreneurs are stuck in the same cycle. Chasing "one day." Always waiting for life to slow down. They say, *"I'm doing this for my family"* or *"I love working,"* but deep down, many are overwhelmed, disconnected, and quietly burning out. They tell themselves that freedom is just around the corner. But the truth is, someday may never come.

That realisation broke my heart. It also forced me to look at myself. I, too, had been doing business the wrong way. I was working non-stop, running on stress, and feeling empty. Eventually, it caught up with me in the form of anxiety. That was my wake-up call.

Six years into business, I hired a life coach, Uma Panch, who helped me slow down, tune in, and completely redefine what success meant. I realised I had been building for the outside world. For approval. For status. For a finish line that kept moving.

Once I reconnected with what I truly valued: my family, my health, my joy, I rebuilt my business and my life from the inside out. That experience made me realise: while there are endless resources on exactly how to grow a business, almost no one teaches you how to grow your life. We've been taught how to create a business plan, but not a life plan.

That's why I wrote this book.

I don't just want to inspire you to live a better life, I want to give you the playbook on how to do exactly that. Because, I know what it's like to feel stuck in survival mode. To be working hard, doing "all the right things," and still feel like you're falling behind. Like your family is getting what's left over instead of your best.

We've all witnessed incredible people.

Brilliant entrepreneurs with big hearts and bigger dreams, pass away far too young. Sudden illness. Unfinished goals. Families left behind. It shook me deeply. Life is fragile.

Tomorrow is never guaranteed. I don't want to wait until it's too late to help someone wake up. I want to shake people out of autopilot now.

Before they miss the moments that matter most.

Today, I live with intention. I have achieved everything I once imagined. A business I can run from anywhere at any time, a luxury home, multiple investment properties, beautiful cars, a marriage of thirteen years that is still passionate, happy, and healthy kids, monthly travel, time for friends, and vibrant health. I share this not to boast, but to show what is possible.

Countless people have asked me how I've designed a life of freedom and fulfilment. I've been invited to speak at EO (Entrepreneurs' Organization) and have had the privilege of mentoring professionals and business owners along the way.

But now, I want to make this message accessible to everyone. This book is the best of what I've lived, learned, and taught. It's systemised into a practical playbook for those ready to build a life of real success.

I know we all want a better life, but most of us were never shown how. We're left to figure it out on our own, and when it feels too hard, we give up. The goal of this book is to make it easier for you to redesign your life. One step at a time.

You don't need to hustle harder. You need to live smarter.

You don't have to wait for freedom. You can design it now.

And you don't have to choose between a thriving business and a meaningful life.

You can have both.

This is my story.

I'm just an ordinary girl who started with nothing, and if I can change my life, so can you.

I hope this book helps you rewrite yours, before it's too late.

Linh 🤍

Section 1. The 360° Success Mindset

"How we spend our days is, of course, how we spend our lives." — Annie Dillard

CHAPTER 1.1

What Does 360° Success Really Mean?

When people think of success, they usually picture the highlight reel: business booming, money flowing, and a lifestyle that looks amazing on the outside.

But most people are like ducks, calm on the surface, while their legs are paddling furiously underwater. They're trying to juggle everything and constantly feeling overwhelmed.

I've met so many entrepreneurs who travel the world, run big businesses, and spend time with family... But their minds are always somewhere else.

They don't sleep well at night. They're not truly present. They're fitting everything in, but it's not intentional. It's not peaceful. Their health takes a back seat.

They don't slow down long enough to breathe, let alone smell the roses.

I know this well because I used to be one of them. Years ago, I felt like I was on a hamster wheel. I was ticking off all the "success" boxes but still waking up feeling unfulfilled.

I couldn't understand why I wasn't truly happy.

That was when I realised I had been focusing so much on building my business, I was neglecting other important areas of my life like my health and my relationships.

And that's when everything changed.

True success isn't just about building a business. It's about building a life you actually love to live, a life that's aligned with your values, your relationships, your peace, and your sense of purpose.

That's where the concept of *360° Success* was born.

360° SUCCESS = WHOLENESS, NOT JUST WEALTH

360° Success is about designing a life that works in every direction, not just financially, but emotionally, spiritually, relationally, and physically.

It's not about perfect balance every day, but about having a *playbook* that helps you come back to alignment when life gets messy (because it will).

That playbook is made up of five key areas I call the Five Pillars of 360° Success. Each pillar reflects a fundamental human need and when nurtured, creates a life that's not just successful, but deeply fulfilling.

Let me walk you through each one, with examples from my own journey.

PILLAR 1. EMPOWERED CONNECTION

"We are wired for connection. Without it, we suffer. With it, we thrive." -Dr. Brené Brown

Connection is more than just being around people, it's about being seen, heard, and understood. It's the bond we form with the people around us: our family, our friends, our community, our clients.

We are biologically designed to thrive through meaningful relationships. In fact, the longest-running study on happiness by Harvard revealed that deep relationships are the number one predictor of long-term health and fulfilment, more than money or success. Without connection, we feel isolated. But with it, we flourish.

Growing up, I didn't feel emotionally connected to my parents. They loved me, but didn't know how to show it in a way I could feel. When I rebelled and became a single mum, that gap became even more obvious.

I was disowned and told not to come back or even speak to my own sister. I didn't have the kind of parental support I needed, so I leaned heavily on my friends. They became my chosen family, supporting me through some of the hardest, loneliest years of my life.

That experience taught me something powerful: we're not meant to do life alone and friends can become the family we choose. Having people to lean on, to encourage you, and to simply show up for you makes all the difference.

One of the most transformational books I've read is *Business Secrets from the Bible* by Rabbi Daniel Lapin. He reminds us that we are all children of God and that God wants us to take care of each other. He also explains that what defines a business is that it has customers, and without customers there is no business.

And in order to have customers, you must solve problems for other people.

In other words, *people are the very lifeblood of your business.* But when you start seeing people as your siblings, fellow children of God, you serve them differently. You listen more.

You give more. You show up with love and integrity. And when you do, you create real value.

And value always leads to financial abundance. Reading this helped me realise something powerful: *Relationships aren't just important in life, they're fundamental to business success too.* We often get caught up in systems, marketing, and strategy, but at the core of everything... it's still people.

When I truly understood this, I stopped hiding behind excuses like "I'm shy" or "I'm too busy." I began prioritising connection not for what I could get, but for what I could *give.* Because business, at its core, is simply an opportunity to serve others well.

In fact, one thing people often say about me is that I'm a natural connector. Over the years, I've built a strong network of friends, business peers, and collaborators, not because I went out "networking," but because I focused on building genuine relationships.

I listen. I show up. I help without expecting anything in return. I've even successfully match-made some friends, and they've been happily married ever since! I have friends from all walks of life and truly enjoy meeting new people. That's why when I need something: an introduction, a referral, a sounding board, I can count on people. Because we're connected, not just acquainted.

If you want to expand your business connections, I highly recommend joining organisations like BNI and EO (Entrepreneurs' Organization). They're fantastic communities to meet like-minded entrepreneurs, build meaningful relationships, and open doors you didn't even know existed.

Remember, when this pillar is strong, you lead from wholeness, not from need.

You connect without an agenda.
You help because you genuinely care.
You attract relationships that lift you higher.
You create value through service, not just strategy.

Empowered Connection is your foundation. It's how you find joy in your work, love in your life, and meaning in your success.

PILLAR 2. BUSINESS FREEDOM

"Your business should give you life, not steal it." -Linh Podetti

Most entrepreneurs start their business for freedom: freedom of time, freedom of choice, freedom from the 9-to-5.

But somewhere along the way, that dream turns into a trap. You end up working longer hours, wearing more hats, and carrying the weight of every decision. Instead of freedom, you find yourself chained to a business that can't run without you. I've seen it first-hand not just in my own journey, but also in my husband's. He built a successful manufacturing business with his brothers for over twenty-five years with over 100 staff.

By all external measures, he'd "made it." But behind the scenes, he was still stuck in the day-to-day: approving orders, solving emergencies, and working twelve hour days. He had the size of success, but not the experience of it. And he's not alone.

I speak to entrepreneurs every week who have built seven, eight, or even nine-figure businesses, but they still can't take a proper holiday. They feel guilty stepping away, or fear the whole thing will collapse without them. That's not business freedom, that's a glorified job with more stress and a bigger payroll.

Business Freedom is about building a business that works for you, not one that constantly needs you. It's about creating a machine that runs *with or without you*, so you can step away and life doesn't fall apart. But it's not just about time.

Business Freedom also includes Financial Freedom. Because what good is a business that runs without you, if it doesn't *pay you* well enough to enjoy your life?

True freedom means having:

- Systems that scale
- People you can trust
- Tools and automation that reduce your workload
- A business model that generates consistent profit
- Enough income to give you real choice in life

When this pillar is strong, your business becomes a platform, not a prison.

It supports your lifestyle instead of competing with it. It funds your dreams instead of draining them. It allows you to be present with your family, generous with your time, and intentional with your energy.

When I first started in business, I was wearing all the hats. I managed marketing, sales, operations, and admin. I thought, *"If I just work harder, I'll get ahead."* But I quickly realised that hustle only took me so far. What helped me break free was outsourcing, documenting my systems, building a team I trust and understanding the financial aspects of business.

I stopped measuring success by how busy I was... and started measuring it by how free I felt.

Later in the book, we'll go much deeper into how to create this kind of business freedom. Because you didn't start your business to own a job. You started it to build a better life.

PILLAR 3: SELF-MASTERY

"You must master yourself before you can lead anyone else." - Zig Ziglar

For a long time, I blamed my circumstances for how I felt.

I blamed my parents for not believing in me.
I blamed the men I dated for how they treated me.
I blamed the business world for being too hard.

But the common thread in all those stories was me. I was reacting to life instead of responding to it. I didn't realise I had the power to change not just my situation, but my inner world. Everything shifted when I finally turned inward and did the work. I began to understand that I needed to master my own-self.

It's recognising that I am the author of my own experience. When I stopped blaming others and took radical responsibility for my mindset, emotions, and behaviours, my life became dramatically more peaceful.

Self-mastery isn't just about mindset. It's about your whole being: body, mind, and soul. You can't lead others, grow a business, or live with intention when you're running on empty.

Your body carries you.

Your mind guides you.

Your soul, nurtured through your relationship with God and your spiritual life, keeps you grounded. When one part is off, everything feels off.

For years, I treated health as something cosmetic and focused only on looking good. But I eventually realised that without real energy and vitality, I couldn't show up for my family, my team, or my purpose. Now, health is a non-negotiable part of my definition of success. I want to feel alive and thriving for as long as possible. I want to be around to watch my grand-kids grow up.

That means:

- Prioritising quality sleep
- Moving my body in ways that feel good, not punishing
- Fuelling myself with nourishing food and hydration
- Making space for rest, reflection, and spiritual connection
- Saying no to what drains me, whether it's people, habits like alcohol, or environments that no longer align

Self-mastery begins with how you treat yourself physically, mentally, and spiritually.

Most entrepreneurs I know understand the physical and mental part of self-mastery. They're great at personal development, goal-setting, and productivity. But where many struggle is with spirituality.

Let me explain what I mean by spirituality.

It's not about religion or rituals. It's about connecting with something bigger than yourself.

It's about strengthening your soul, your inner world, and staying grounded no matter what's happening around you. One truth I've come to believe deeply is this: we are spiritual beings having a physical experience.

Our bodies are temporary. Our spirit is eternal.

Even science supports this. Research in quantum physics and studies of near-death experiences suggest that our consciousness, our awareness, exists beyond the physical body. Scholars like Dr. Gary Schwartz and Dr. Bruce Greyson have found compelling evidence that our spirit continues on, beyond the limits of the body.

Understanding this changed everything for me.

Self-mastery is not just about success in this life. It's about tending to the part of you that outlives your to-do list, your business, and your achievements. It's about being anchored in something eternal.

One of the biggest turning points in my self-mastery journey was discovering my faith. Before faith, I thought I had to carry everything myself. Plan it all. Control it all. Solve it all.

But faith taught me a different way. Through prayer, reading the Bible, and staying connected to my church community, I learned to let go of the illusion of control. I began handing my worries over to God, trusting that even when I couldn't see progress, He was still working.

The daily habits of prayer, studying Scripture, and staying rooted in my faith helped me stay calm through challenges that once would have overwhelmed me. I realised that true leadership isn't about striving harder.

It's about surrendering deeper.

In short, self-mastery is the bridge between who you are today and who you're meant to become. It sets the foundation for leading others. If you can't lead yourself, you can't lead anyone else.

When your body feels good, your mind becomes clear.
When your mind is clear, your decisions improve.
When your soul is anchored in God's truth, your leadership becomes powerful.

PILLAR 4. FAMILY BALANCE

"No success in business is worth failure at home." - David O. Mckay

For years, I thought being around my kids was enough. I took them to school, cooked their meals, and was physically present. But mentally? Emotionally? I was miles away juggling emails, putting out fires, glued to my phone. I was multitasking motherhood and entrepreneurship, convincing myself I was doing both well. But the truth was: I was giving my family the leftovers of me, not the best of me.

They deserved more than just proximity.

They deserved presence.

As a Vietnamese woman married to an Italian man, both cultures are *big* on family. I grew up with the saying that "family is everything," and I've carried that into adulthood. But building a business often pulls you away from the very people you're doing it for. That's the paradox many entrepreneurs face.

Once my business began to thrive, I realised I had a rare gift: the ability to choose how I spend my time. And I chose family. Not just my husband and kids, but also my parents, in-laws, and extended relatives.

I started organising annual holidays with my parents and in-laws, knowing those moments wouldn't last forever.

I planned weekends away with cousins and aunties just to bond and make memories.

I scheduled one-on-one getaways with each of my kids to build lifelong connections with them.

Financial success gave me the means, but *intention* gave me the motivation. This isn't always about grand gestures. It's about little decisions that add up. Choosing to put the phone away during dinner or saying no to meetings after 3pm so I could be present at school pickup. One of the greatest joys in my life now is knowing that my business doesn't just provide for my family, it gives me the *time* to enjoy them. To pour into them. To show up.

And let's be real, this isn't always easy.

There are still times when work demands attention, or when the lines blur. But I've built a rhythm and system that helps me come back to centre, to realign. I don't strive for perfect balance every day, I strive for intentional connection over time.

Family Balance isn't about being the perfect parent, child, or partner. It's about *showing up intentionally.* About making space in your calendar, your mind, and your heart for the people who matter most.

PILLAR 5. LIFE EXPERIENCES

"You weren't made to just work and pay bills. You were made to live." - Linh Podetti

I didn't grow up with holidays or joyful experiences. Life was about survival, doing what needed to be done, getting through school, and helping the family. There wasn't space for fun, celebration, or dreaming beyond the day-to-day.

That upbringing shaped my beliefs early on. For years, I believed that fun had to be earned. That joy was only allowed after the work was done. That holidays and rest were indulgences, not necessities. And every time I tried to relax, guilt would creep in. *"Shouldn't I be doing something more productive?"*

But eventually, I began to shift. I noticed that when I took time off, when I travelled and explored new places, I came back more energised, more creative, and more connected to life. Life experiences weren't distractions from growth, they *fuelled* it. Life isn't meant to be postponed.

We say we'll go on that trip "when the business settles," or we'll take a break "after the next launch." But there's always another project. Another client. Another goal. And the truth is, you don't get those moments back. No one looks back and says, *"I'm so glad I skipped all those holidays so I could keep up with my inbox."* They say, *"I wish I spent more time with the people I love. I wish I made more memories."*

When you prioritise life experiences, you don't just create joy, you create legacy. Because at your funeral, no one will care how much money you made or what kind of car you drove. They'll remember how you made them feel. The fun you had together. The memories you created.

My husband is a classic example. He often says, *"I don't need holidays."* But at the end of each year, I always ask him, *"What were your top highlights?"* And without fail, he names all the holidays we went on. Not the work wins. Not the income goals. Instead, he mentions the getaways, the fun times and the memories.

That moment always reminds me of something powerful: When you buy things, they feel tangible, but you quickly forget them. When you invest in experiences, they feel intangible but they stay with you forever.

This is why I believe so deeply in designing a life rich with meaningful moments. It's not about luxury, it's about intention. Fun, joy, and rest aren't rewards for working hard. They're essential ingredients for a fulfilling life.

In a later chapter, you'll learn how to create your own Bucket List for Life. I'll guide you through how to design experiences with your partner, kids, family, or friends so you're not just building a business, but building a life you actually want to remember. The goal is simple:

To be busy having fun.
To be fully present.
To create memories you'll talk about for the rest of your life.

Because at the end of the day, that's what you'll remember. And that's what they'll remember about you.

WHY THESE 5 PILLARS MATTER

In a world that glorifies hustle, comparison, and burnout, 360° Success calls you back to wholeness. It reminds you that:

- You are more than your productivity.
- Your worth is not tied to your calendar.
- Success is not just what you build, it's how you feel while building it.

This framework doesn't just help you grow your business. It helps you build a life you don't want to escape from. In the next chapter, we'll explore why traditional models of success often leave us feeling empty and how you can break free from that cycle to create a business and life that truly fulfil you.

SELF ASSESSMENT

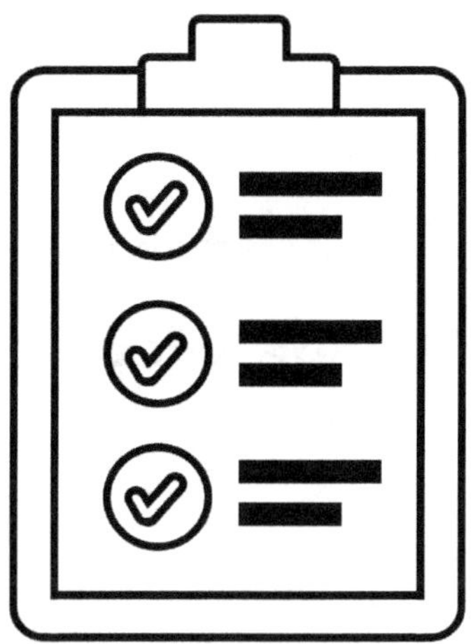

To bring awareness to the areas of your life that might need more focus, head to linhpodetti.com and take the 360° Success Quiz. This quick and free quiz helps you reflect on how you're doing across the five key pillars of life:

Empowered Connection, Business Freedom, Self-Mastery, Family Balance, and Life Experiences.

You'll get a simple overview of where you're thriving and where there's room for improvement plus helpful suggestions on what to start paying attention to.

This is a great starting point to help you live more intentionally and take your next step toward 360° Success.

Take the quiz now at **linhpodetti.com**.

CHAPTER 1.2

Why Traditional Success Isn't Enough

We've been sold a narrow definition of success. From a young age, we're taught that success looks like working hard, climbing the ladder, earning more, buying property, and maybe if you're lucky, retiring comfortably one day.

And as entrepreneurs, that script often shifts into: *Grow fast. Make millions. Be everywhere. Scale big. Don't stop.*

I often get sidetracked and fall for this too. But I always remind myself of these truths:

- You can achieve all of that and still feel unfulfilled.
- You can hit your revenue goals and still feel anxious.
- You can have the perfect-looking life and still feel like something's missing.

I know, because I've been there.

WHEN "SUCCESS" BECOMES A TRAP

There was a point in my life when, from the outside, it looked like I had it all together:

- A 7-figure business
- A global team
- Flexibility to travel
- A beautiful family

And yet, I found myself asking:
"Why do I still feel behind?"
"Why am I constantly overwhelmed, even though I've ticked so many boxes?"

Here's what I came to realise: I was chasing a version of success that wasn't even mine, it was shaped by other people's values.

I was constantly comparing myself to others, feeling like I was behind, even when I was doing well. I became obsessed with getting there faster, cutting corners, skipping rest, and trying to force progress.

That's when it hit me: *Traditional success is often external. But true success? It's internal.*

It's not just about what we build, it's about who we're becoming in the process. And if the process robs us of peace, joy, and meaning... is it really success at all?

THE FISHERMAN AND THE BUSINESSMAN

There's an old parable that illustrates this beautifully: A wealthy businessman was visiting a small coastal village when he saw a fisherman relaxing by his boat.

The businessman asked,

"Why aren't you out fishing longer?"

The fisherman replied,

"I've caught enough for today. I spend the rest of my time playing music, napping, and enjoying my family."

The businessman said,

"But if you fished more, you could buy a bigger boat. Then you could catch more fish, hire workers, open a factory... eventually, you could be rich!"

The fisherman asked,

"Then what?"

The businessman proudly replied,

"Then you could retire and do what you love... relax, play music, and enjoy your family."

The fisherman smiled.

"But I'm already doing that now."

That story is a powerful reminder: *We often chase more, thinking it will give us what we already have access to.* The peace, the joy, the connection, it's available when we choose a different definition of success.

THE FLAWED MODEL OF TRADITIONAL SUCCESS

Let's break it down. The traditional model of success is often rooted in:

- Busyness = Importance
- More = Better
- Sacrifice now = Joy later
- Productivity = Worth

But this model is broken.

- Being busy doesn't mean you're doing what matters.
- Earning more doesn't guarantee you're living well.
- Sacrificing your health, family, or joy for a distant future often means you never truly enjoy the present.
- And your worth has never been tied to how much you can do in a day.

This mindset leads to what many now call:

"High-performance emptiness" and it's a silent epidemic among entrepreneurs. Even psychologist Dr. Tal Ben-Shahar, who taught Harvard's most popular course on happiness, found that many high-achieving students were suffering from anxiety, burnout, and a deep sense of emptiness.

Why? Because they were chasing success that excluded emotional, relational, and spiritual well-being.

The entrepreneurial world is no exception. Studies show that 72% of entrepreneurs report mental health concerns, including anxiety, depression, and burnout.

In fact, entrepreneurs are twice as likely to suffer from depression, and tragically, suicide rates among business owners are higher than in the general population.

The pressure to perform, succeed, and "keep it all together" silently crushes many behind the scenes.

This same warning is echoed in *Die With Zero* book by Bill Perkins, where he challenges the idea of endlessly accumulating wealth while postponing joy.

Too many people delay truly living only to discover, when they finally make time for it, that the spark has faded, or worse that it's too late.

THE DEEPER SHIFT: FROM DOING TO BECOMING

For most of my life, I was focused on outcomes. I'd set the next big goal, hit it, then immediately move onto the next. It was a constant cycle of chasing, achieving, and repeating. But somewhere along the way, I started feeling tired not just physically, but deep in my soul.

Even as things looked "successful" on the outside, I couldn't shake the question that kept bubbling up: Is this it? That's when I came across a message from Pastor Vlad Savchuk, the pastor who actually introduced me to my Christian faith.

He said something that completely re-framed how I saw success:

> *"God is far more interested in who you're becoming than what you're achieving."*

That line hit me hard. And whether you call it God, the universe, your inner compass, or a higher purpose, that truth still holds: The real goal isn't to chase success.

The real goal is to please God and become someone of substance, someone who lives with integrity, purpose, and strong character, in alignment with their higher power.

Instead of asking, *"What can I achieve next?"*
I now ask, *"Who am I becoming in the process?"*

That one internal shift changed everything. Life became more meaningful. I no longer felt like I was sprinting toward a finish line I couldn't see.

I began measuring success not by what I had done, but by who I was becoming day by day, moment by moment.

And it's a question I still ask myself today.

Because when you focus on becoming the kind of person you'd be proud to follow, everything else begins to align: your habits, your relationships, your business, and even your sense of peace.

FROM "DOING" GOALS TO "BEING" GOALS

Most of us are conditioned to set action-based goals:

- "I want to lose 10kg."
- "I want to make $1 million."
- "I want to raise well-behaved kids."
- "I want to build a best-selling brand."

But here's the problem:

Doing goals are destination-focused. Once you hit them, you're often left wondering, now what?

Instead, what if we started setting *being goal*, goals rooted in identity and alignment?

Inspired by *Atomic Habits* book by James Clear, identity-based goals sound like this:

- "I want to become someone who values their health *and* honours their body daily."
- "I want to become a calm *and* present parent who leads with love and patience."
- "I want to be a business owner who creates opportunity, serves others, *and* lives in alignment with my values."
- "I want to be a person who creates lasting impact, not just income."

When your identity is strong, your behaviour naturally aligns. And when who you are matches what you do, that's when life starts to feel whole.

YOU DON'T ATTRACT WHAT YOU WANT, YOU ATTRACT WHO YOU ARE

Here's a truth I've seen play out over and over again in my life and in others: You don't attract what you want, you attract what you are.

If you want a kind, loyal partner: become one.

If you want to build a trustworthy team: become a leader worth trusting.

If you want to attract calmness and clarity: live with it yourself first.

It always starts with who you're becoming, not just what you're achieving.

A NEW DEFINITION OF WINNING

Let's stop obsessing over performance and start becoming people we'd be proud to follow. Here's what winning looks like through the lens of 360° Success:

- Running a profitable business and being emotionally present at dinner
- Travelling the world and staying grounded in your values
- Building a team and nurturing your marriage
- Making time for creativity, rest, and faith, not just constant hustle

You don't have to choose between impact and inner peace. Between ambition and alignment. Between growth and grace. You can have both.

REDEFINE YOUR LEGACY

One day, all of our lives will be reduced to a dash between two dates. What will yours represent? When I think about my final days, I don't want to be remembered for how much money I made or how many followers I had.

I want to be remembered for how I made people feel.

That I was kind.

That I helped others rise.

That I honoured my values.

That I lived a life that pleased God and felt good to live.

Let 360° Success be your permission slip to slow down, align, and live on purpose. Because you weren't just made to do more. You were made to become more.

REFLECTION PROMPTS

Take a moment to pause and journal:

1. Am I chasing external achievements or becoming the person I truly want to be?
2. What would a fulfilling, peaceful, and meaningful version of success look like for me?
3. What new identity do you want to embody? Write a new declaration: *E.g. "I am someone who protects my peace and leads with purpose."*
4. What is the one daily action you can do to ensure you're embodying your new identity? *E.g. Meditating for 10 mins a day.*

CHAPTER 1.3

When Is Enough Truly Enough?

Why do entrepreneurs want more money? It's a question I've asked myself and many others over and over again. The drive to build, grow, and earn is at the core of most entrepreneurs. But what happens when you've built a successful business, and you're still chasing more? One of my friends is a perfect example. He's built a $50 million business and is now focused on reaching $100 million.

On the surface, it's an inspiring story of ambition and scale. But behind the scenes, his wife is frustrated, his kids are growing up without him, and he's missing out on the very life he claims to be building for his family.

He's not alone. Many entrepreneurs reach a level of success that most people would dream of and then move the goalposts. Instead of asking, *"What do I want life to look like?"* They ask, *"How do I double the revenue?"* The problem is, they're already financially free.

The business is no longer just about survival, it's about ego, competition, or habit. Often, they don't even realise it.

A REALITY CHECK: HOW WEALTHY ARE YOU REALLY?

Most entrepreneurs don't stop to realise just how wealthy they already are. We're so busy chasing the next milestone that we rarely pause to assess where we actually stand.

So let's ground this conversation in some real numbers.

- Globally, to be in the top 1% of wealth, you need a net worth of just USD $1.2 million (around AUD $1.85 million).
- In Australia, the top 1% net worth threshold is around AUD $7.18 million. And to be in the top 1% of income earners, a combined household income (you and your partner) of around AUD $531,652 per year is required.
- In the United States, you'd need a net worth of approximately USD $11.2 million to be in the top 1%, and a combined household income of about USD $787,712 per year.

If you're already close to or beyond these numbers, you're not just doing well, you're in the global elite. You're wealthier than 99% of humanity.

So the question isn't whether you need more, but whether you're actually enjoying what you've built.

Many entrepreneurs, even those who have crossed this global 1% mark, still feel like they're behind. Now, you might be thinking, *"But I haven't hit the 1% in my country yet."* That's okay. Because here's the deeper truth:

Financial freedom doesn't start when you hit an arbitrary number. It starts when you shift your mindset from chasing *more* to appreciating *enough.*

Many people who never reach millionaire status still live rich, joyful, meaningful lives. And many people with millions feel stressed, empty, and disconnected. The real benchmark isn't how much you make, it's how intentionally you use your money to create peace, presence, and purpose while you build.

THE TRAP OF LIFESTYLE INFLATION

One of my all-time favourite documentaries is *Minimalism.*

It explores how we often buy far more than we need and how that creates unnecessary stress.

There's one line that really stuck with me: *"The more money we make, the more stuff we buy."* That simple truth gave a name to something I'd experienced myself and witnessed in so many others. It's called *lifestyle inflation.*

As our income grows, so does our spending. I've seen friends who earn less than me, yet their pantries are stocked for a year, their homes are filled with toys in every room, and their wardrobes overflow with clothes. It's not always about the money, it's about filling our lives with *stuff* instead of *meaning*.

And I've been there too. As my business grew, I started justifying bigger expenses.

I remember buying my first expensive handbag. It felt good... but not for long. Soon, I felt like I needed another one. After purchasing several bags costing me tens of thousands of dollars, I realised I was spending money on things that didn't actually make me happy (at least, not for long).

We often mistake buying for living, and clutter for success.

Just because we can have more doesn't mean we *should*. The cost isn't just financial, it's mental and emotional too.

The *Minimalism* documentary also pointed out that too much stuff doesn't just clutter our homes, it clutters our minds. Studies show that clutter can increase cortisol (the stress hormone), reduce focus, and even impair sleep.

Excess possessions often lead to decision fatigue, anxiety, and a never-ending cycle of needing more. The more you accumulate, the more time and energy it takes to manage, maintain, and organise. In reality, our *stuff* can start to own us.

I began de-cluttering, room by room and with each space cleared, I felt more peace and clarity. I started investing my hard-earned money not on things, but on memories: beautiful holidays, glamorous parties, and shared moments with family and friends that we'll cherish forever.

Dave Ramsey famously said,

> *"We buy things we don't need with money we don't have to impress people we don't like."*

We work long hours, hustle endlessly, and sacrifice time with loved ones... all to fund a lifestyle we think we *should* have. But here's the truth: if we stop buying things we don't actually need, we wouldn't have to work so hard just to keep up. Less stuff means less pressure, less debt, and more freedom.

What if the real flex isn't what you own, but how much peace you have?

WHEN GROWTH STOPS FEELING GOOD

Let me share a bit of my own journey.

When I first started my business, I thought making $250K would be life-changing. It felt like the dream. And it was... until it wasn't.

I reached that goal, and suddenly $1 million became the new benchmark. I hired more staff, served more clients, and the business kept growing. But so did the grind.

I was chasing growth for growth's sake. I wanted to move faster, scale bigger, and hit the next milestone. But as I scaled, profit margins got squeezed. I remember my husband who runs a manufacturing business once said to me, *"Even with an 8-figure business, sometimes I preferred when it was half the size. Less headache, fewer people to manage."* And he was right.

Bigger doesn't always mean better. More revenue can mean more stress, lower profit, and less time to enjoy life. Growth can be beautiful, but only if it serves your life, not consumes it. I'm not against money. I believe in building wealth, creating jobs, and enjoying the fruits of your labour. But if you've already built something successful, and life still feels hollow, ask yourself:

- Is your next financial goal truly necessary?
- Would your life really change if you made $2M more?
- What would you do differently today if you already had enough?

The truth is, many of us could live our dream life right now, we're just caught in an outdated mindset.

We think success is about numbers. But success is about alignment.

THE SCIENCE: DOES MORE MONEY MAKE YOU HAPPIER?

Numerous studies have tackled the money versus happiness debate. According to a 2010 Princeton University study, happiness increases with income but only up to about USD $75,000 a year.

After that, the emotional benefits of more money tend to level off. More recent research by Matthew Killingsworth (2021) suggests happiness can continue rising with income but only if you actually enjoy the work you're doing. If your work is draining or unaligned, no amount of money will make you feel fulfilled.

The real takeaway? Money helps up to a point. After that, it's what you do with your time, your health, your relationships, and how aligned your life feels that determines real happiness.

And here's the irony: today, the world's richest people are intentionally doing the very things that poor people have always done to survive.

- *They plunge into ice cold water to build resilience.*
- *They fast for days to improve health and discipline.*
- *They strip things back to the basics, seeking simplicity in wellness, food, and lifestyle.*

In the past, the poor had no choice but to live simply; cold baths, little food, basic shelter. Now, despite having access to anything money can buy, the wealthy are choosing these uncomfortable habits to feel stronger and more alive.

And then there's the ultra-wealthy, with far more money than they could ever need. Some spend $5,000 on a single shot of Louis XIII Cognac or indulge in rare caviar that, truthfully, many don't even enjoy. The value isn't in the flavour, it's in the exclusivity. It's about being one of the few in the world who can say they've had it. At a certain point, luxury stops being about enjoyment and becomes a performance of status.

The truth is, we were never designed to live in constant excess. We were designed to thrive on discipline, simplicity, gratitude, and meaningful living.

WHEN GROWTH BECOMES A DISTRACTION

We often say we're building our businesses to create freedom and to be happy. But many of us find ourselves trapped in a cycle of never-ending more. It's easy to fall into the pattern:

- *Hire more staff*
- *Add more products*
- *Open more locations*
- *Scale faster*

And somewhere along the way... we lose our joy.

If you're honest with yourself, sometimes growth isn't about strategy, it's a distraction from the discomfort of stillness.

We don't know how to just *be*, so we build. We don't feel successful unless we're *busy*, so we keep adding.

But the true work of a fulfilled entrepreneur isn't more hustle. It's *clarity*.

THE REAL QUESTION: WHAT IS THIS ALL FOR?

There are countless examples of incredibly successful entrepreneurs who reached extraordinary levels of wealth, yet missed out on the fullness of life.

Take Steve Jobs, for example. He built one of the most influential companies in the world and died with a net worth in the billions. But in the end, even he acknowledged that wealth means little without health and meaningful connection.

Consider media mogul Rupert Murdoch, one of the wealthiest and most influential men in the world, yet his life has been marked by multiple divorces and public family conflicts over power and succession.

Also Elon Musk, one of the most brilliant minds of our time, with multiple companies and children, but also a history of broken relationships, family complexity, and relentless work that raises questions about the cost of such success. These are reminders that ambition without boundaries can come at a devastating cost.

Money alone does not protect us from burnout, regret, or broken relationships.

The real goal should be to build a business that enhances your life, not one that slowly consumes it.

MAKING ROOM FOR WHAT MATTERS

Let me be clear, I'm all for making more money. I still have ambitious financial goals. In fact, I want to 10X my business over the next five years. But here's the difference: I'm not willing to sacrifice my happiness in other areas of life just to get there.

I've learned that before you double down on business growth, you must first carve out time for the parts of life that truly make it rich:

> your health, your family, your friendships,
> your faith, your peace.

If you're honouring those areas, then by all means, go all in with the time that's left. Build the business. Grow it fast if you want to. But do it from a place of wholeness, not burnout.

It's not *"when this happens, then I'll be happy."*
It's *"I'm living a happy life while I pursue my goals."*

And if that 10X goal doesn't happen in five years? Maybe it'll take ten. Who said it has to be a sprint? Your life doesn't start when you hit the goal, it's happening right now. Don't trade the best parts of it for a number on a spreadsheet.

WHAT'S REALLY DRIVING YOU?

Entrepreneurs often tell me, *"But I just love the game of business. I love working."* And I get it, I used to say the same thing. But through my own personal development journey, I discovered something deeper.

Sometimes, that love for the hustle is really just a mask for unresolved trauma.

A fear of not being enough.
A fear of not being loved unless we achieve.

For many years, I was unknowingly driven by a need to prove myself to my parents, to show them I was capable. That I was worthy. It wasn't until I worked with my life coach, Uma, that I began to confront those beliefs.

And I realised: I didn't need more success to be enough... I already was!

The only way to truly understand what's driving us is to do the inner work.

To face the past, uncover hidden self-sabotage, and

release the limiting beliefs we often don't even realise are there.

For me, that journey wouldn't be possible without the help of Uma. She patiently guides me through the layers of past experiences and unresolved trauma, helping me break free from what no longer serves me. If you're serious about growth, I highly recommend investing in yourself and working with a trusted professional. It's one of the most powerful decisions you can make.

And let me emphasise this clearly. There is nothing wrong with ambition. But the healthiest form of ambition comes from *self-worth*, not *insecurity.*

Wanting more while being detached from the outcome is the goal. Building something great while also being present for the people you love... that is the real win!

WHEN BUSINESS BECOMES AN ADDICTION

As adults, we often shake our heads at kids glued to their screens, playing video games for hours on end. We complain they've lost touch with the real world, forgetting to eat, sleep, or engage with their families. And tragically, this isn't just about wasted time.

There have been real stories of teenagers dying from dehydration and exhaustion after marathon gaming sessions. They were so locked into the pursuit of points, levels, and digital wins that they forgot their most basic needs.

But here's the hard truth: many of us are no different.

Business is a game too and a dangerously addictive one. Each sale, client win, or financial milestone becomes a dopamine hit. We call it "the hustle," but really, we're just levelling up like gamers, chasing more coins, more followers, more zeros in the bank. And just like those kids, we can become so immersed in the game that we forget to eat well, nurture relationships, or rest. We justify it by saying we're doing it "for the family," but if we're never present with them, who are we really doing it for?

We can't criticise kids for being obsessed with games if we're playing one too, only ours is called business. The scoreboard might be different, but the consequences can be eerily similar. Burnout. Health issues. Estranged relationships. Missed memories. All because we didn't know when to press pause.

The real game isn't about reaching the next level. It's about learning when to step away from the screen and be here. With the people you love. In the body you've been given. In the moment that's happening now.

REDEFINING THE WEALTH GAME

This chapter is an invitation to redefine the game. Especially if you're no longer in survival mode, you owe it to yourself and your family to pause and recalibrate.

1. What does enough look like to you?
2. What does success look like beyond the spreadsheet?
3. What would make you feel more present, more alive, more connected?

You didn't start your business to become a prisoner to it. You started it for freedom. In the next section 2. called "Laying the Foundation", we'll shift gears and begin laying the foundation for your 360° success journey: starting with clarity, values, and vision. Because before you can build a life and business that align, you need to know exactly what you're building toward.

ACTION STEPS

1. **Journal:** What would I do if I had all the money I needed?
2. **Identify:** What am I chasing, and why?
3. **Reflect:** What's one area of life I've been neglecting in the name of growth?
4. **Decide:** What does "enough" look like for me right now?

CHAPTER 1.4

Facing the Inevitable: Mortality

How remembering death can help you start truly living.

You woke up today. That's a blessing. But did you know that over 150,000 people in the world didn't? In Australia, around 480 people die every single day. In the U.S., that number climbs to over 8,300 per day. Many were healthy. Many were young. Many had plans for the weekend. Some had dinner defrosting, emails half-written, goals half-done. They didn't know it was their last sunrise.

We don't like to think about death, let alone talk about it. Especially in the world of business and success, where we're focused on growth, plans, and the future. But what if death was the most powerful motivator we've been avoiding? What if facing our mortality, not in a morbid way, but in a real, grounded way...was exactly what we need to snap out of autopilot and start living with meaning, not just momentum?

I've seen it first-hand. Not just in statistics, but in the stories of people I knew.

One of my husband's long-time staff, a loyal and hard-working man, was diagnosed with cancer suddenly and gone just six weeks later. He didn't get a long goodbye or a retirement party. He got a quick ending. He was only 48 years old and had a 6 year old son.

More recently, a fellow entrepreneur from my Entrepreneurs' Organization (EO) community died suddenly, while on a treadmill. Surprisingly, he was also 48. Fit. Strong. Full of energy and goals. One moment, he was training. The next, gone.

These moments shake you. Because they shatter the illusion that time is promised. They remind us that we are not in control of the clock.

THE RELATIONSHIP SIDE OF MORTALITY

Facing mortality isn't just about our health. It's about our relationships. It's about realising that our parents may not be around much longer.

That "someday" catch-up with your old friend might not happen. That your kids are growing up every second and one day, you'll carry them for the last time without even realising it. We often talk about success in terms of business milestones, but we measure loss in moments, the time we didn't take, the words we didn't say, the presence we didn't give.

It's not just about how long we live, but how fully we love while we're here.

REGRETS OF THE DYING

Australian palliative care nurse Bronnie Ware famously wrote in her book about the top five regrets of the dying. Among them:

1. *"I wish I hadn't worked so hard."*
2. *"I wish I had stayed in touch with my friends."*
3. *"I wish I had let myself be happier."*

Nobody said, *"I wish I hit one more business goal"* or *"I wish I spent more time in the office."* Their regrets were about connection, presence, and joy.

This message resonated so deeply with me that I made it part of the speech at my 10-year wedding vow renewal party in 2022.

We gathered with 100 guests to celebrate not just our anniversary, but the gift of love, life, and togetherness. At first, my husband was against the idea, like many people might be.

He thought it would be easier (and cheaper) to just go on a holiday together. He said we'd already gotten married once, so why do it again? But I saw it differently. I saw it as a beautiful opportunity to celebrate our love and bring our loved ones together.

Money well spent. Memories well made.

And guess what? My husband changed his mind. He loved it. Even more special, our kids got to witness us renewing our vows, something they missed the first time, because they hadn't been born yet.

In my speech, I said, *"Sure, I could've gone on a holiday with my husband to mark this milestone. But then 100 of you wouldn't have been part of it. And I would've missed the chance to create these memories with you."*

THE REGRETS ENTREPRENEURS DON'T TALK ABOUT

This message was echoed powerfully in a conversation I had with Travis Luther, a fellow EO member in Colorado on my EO Business Podcast. After losing his father to addiction, Travis realised he never got the closure or wisdom he needed.

So, he began interviewing people in hospice care, asking the big questions many of us avoid until it's too late:

What do you regret?
What do you wish you had done differently?

Their responses were raw and deeply human. They didn't talk about revenue, resumes, or what they achieved. They talked about what they abandoned. Many had spent their lives living up to others' expectations, chasing approval, or doing what was "right" instead of what was real. One man told Travis, *"There was a life I truly wanted, but somewhere along the way I lost it."*

They spoke about authenticity. Missed relationships. Time they gave away to people who didn't value it. Versions of themselves they buried under obligation. And that's when it hit me: we're not just running out of time, we're often running the wrong race.

Travis found a common theme among entrepreneurs too. Many of us throw ourselves into work not because we're chasing a vision, but because we're avoiding something. Unprocessed trauma. Strained relationships. Disconnection. It's a productive form of escape. We tell ourselves we're building a better future but often, we're numbing the present.

One of the most sobering insights from Travis's research? Many of the people he interviewed were young. In their 30s, 40s. Fit. Successful. And still, out of nowhere, received a devastating diagnosis. Their message for the rest of us?

> Don't wait.
> Don't wait to speak your truth.
> Don't wait to say "I love you."
> Don't wait to align your life with what actually matters to you.
> Don't wait until the treadmill moment, the diagnosis, the tragedy.

As Travis put it, *"Money can't buy your time back. Or your peace. Or your health. So use it now... to live, to connect, to love."*

LET DEATH AWAKEN YOU, NOT SCARE YOU

I don't want you to be afraid of death. I want you to be awake to life.

To live like it matters.
To speak the words now, not later.
To take the trip, hug your mum, delete the app that's stealing your minutes.
To stop wasting time proving yourself to people who don't matter.

Facing our mortality isn't dark. It's freeing. It wakes us up. Because when you know your time is limited, you start treating it like gold, not confetti.

And the best part? You don't need to wait for a wake-up call from life. This is your wake-up call! Right here. Right now.

Remember this...

"The most successful life is not the one with the biggest income, but the one with the fewest regrets."

REFLECTION PROMPTS

Take 5 minutes now and answer these:

1. Who in your life would you deeply regret not spending time with if they were gone tomorrow?
2. What have you been putting off because you think you have time?
3. If you died tomorrow, what would you hope people say about you?
4. What can you do today to make that true?

CHAPTER 1.5

Understanding the Seasons of Life

Life comes in seasons.

Spring ❀
Summer ☼
Autumn 🍂
Winter ❄

It's not just a rhythm we see in nature, it's a rhythm we live through as human beings. Understanding the season you're in brings self-awareness, peace, and permission to evolve. It helps you release old expectations and embrace what this moment of life is really asking of you.

Yet most of us were never taught to see life this way. We compare ourselves across seasons.

We judge ourselves unfairly. We wonder why we feel so different than we did ten years ago and think something must be wrong. But nothing is wrong. You're just in a *new season.*

THE FOUR SEASONS OF LIFE

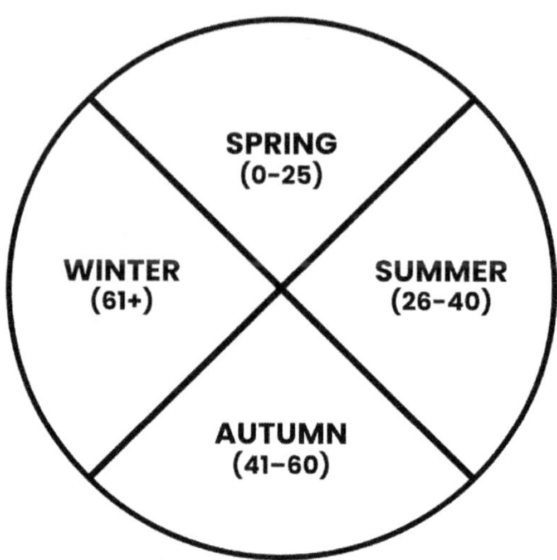

The concept of life as a cycle of seasons has been explored by thinkers like Jim Rohn, who used seasonal metaphors to teach life and business wisdom. Authors like Brian Tracy and even ancient philosophies have echoed this truth: we grow in cycles. And when we work with them, not against them, we thrive. Here's one way to understand them:

1. Spring (0–25 years old): Discovery & Learning

   The season of exploration, play, trial and error. You're figuring out who you are, what excites you, what hurts, and what helps. There's an energy of becoming and potential.

2. Summer (26–40 years old): Achievement & Building

   A time of drive and creation: career, family, identity, income. It's busy. It's demanding. You're working hard to build the life you pictured. Often, success and busyness go hand in hand.

3. Autumn (41–60 years old): Meaning & Contribution

   You begin to slow down, but not because you're tired, but because you're starting to think more deeply. Is this it? What really matters now? You want your work to feel meaningful. You want your time to matter. You're not chasing more, you're searching for better.

4. Winter (61+ years old): Reflection & Wisdom

   A time of distilling what really counts. You give more generously, mentor others, and find joy in simplicity. You look back with clarity. Ideally, you rest in peace, not because life is over, but because you've lived it well.

WHY YOUR 40'S CAN FEEL LIKE A CRISIS (BUT ISN'T)

Many people in their 40's begin to feel a shift and panic. You're no longer excited by the same goals. You've achieved things you thought would make you happy... but feel strangely unfulfilled.

You might feel lost, flat, or question everything:
Your marriage, career, identity, purpose.

This is common. And it's not a crisis, it's an awakening. You're entering *Autumn*, a time of reflection, integration, and redefinition.

You start wanting less clutter, fewer masks, and more alignment. You want to love more deeply.

Work more intentionally. Live more truthfully. And if you're feeling that now, I want you to know:

You're not failing.
You're just waking up.

STOP COMPARING SEASONS

One of the most damaging things we can do is compare ourselves to others in different seasons of life. You're not meant to have the energy of a 25-year-old in your 40's. You're not supposed to be "crushing it" 24/7 if your soul is asking you to slow down. Know your season. Honour your season. This is how we make peace with our pace.

Spring and Summer are seasons of *doing.*
Autumn and Winter are seasons of *being.*

This shift can be uncomfortable, especially for high achievers. You've built an identity around productivity, winning, and results.

But now, your inner voice is whispering something deeper. It's asking:

- Who are you without the hustle?
- What is the meaning of life?
- What truly makes you happy?
- What legacy are you creating?

These aren't distractions. These are the real questions.

And if you're brave enough to sit with them, they'll lead you somewhere beautiful.

MY PERSONAL JOURNEY: FROM RESTLESS TO ROOTED

When I entered my mid-30's, I found myself in the middle of a shift. From the outside, I had success: business growth, a beautiful family, and a life I once dreamed about.

But inside, something was stirring — a quiet discontent, a longing for something deeper. I began asking myself:

What's the point of all this?
Is this really the life I want to live?

Those questions led me down a surprising path, one I never expected. I found myself exploring faith. And eventually, I gave my life to Jesus.

This might surprise you, because I didn't grow up religious. In fact, I used to be an atheist. I believed in working hard, doing good, and relying only on myself. But the deeper I searched for purpose, the more I realised there was something beyond me. Call it God, call it the Universe, whatever you call it, the experience was life-changing.

My journey towards faith has become the foundation of how I live, lead, parent, and make decisions. It has given me a peace I never had, a compass when I feel lost, and a purpose that goes far beyond profit.

I'm not sharing this to preach. I'm sharing it because it's what helped me when I didn't know what else to reach for. And if you're in your own season of questioning, I want you to know it's okay. You're not alone. And I hope you find the truth that anchors you, too.

FINAL THOUGHTS

Life isn't linear.

It's seasonal.

When you understand what season you're in, everything begins to make more sense.

Mid-life isn't a breakdown. It's an invitation. To go deeper. To let go of what no longer serves you. To live not by default, but by design.

ACTION STEPS

1. Which season of life are you in right now? How does that help you make sense of what you're feeling?
2. What parts of your identity or habits feel ready to be shed?
3. What are you being called to step into in this season, whether that's rest, impact, service, or stillness?
4. What's something you've been avoiding that may be worth exploring spiritually, relationally, or personally?

Section 2. Laying the Foundation

"Efforts and courage are not enough without purpose and direction." — John F. Kennedy

CHAPTER 2.1

Define Your Personal and Business Vision

As entrepreneurs, we are used to setting goals and visions for our business. It is what we do. But rarely do we take the time to create a vision for our life.

We spend so much energy building the business, that life quietly takes the back seat, until one day, we realise we have built something impressive, yet feel unfulfilled.

But what if we flipped the script? What if we started by defining the kind of life we want, and then designed a business that supports it? That is what this chapter is about. It is about creating the clarity needed to achieve 360° Success.

It is time to stop living in autopilot mode and start leading your life and business with intention. Because if you do not know where you are going, how will you know if you have arrived?

YOU ARE THE ARCHITECT OF YOUR LIFE

Think of your life as a dream home. Would you ever build it without a floor plan? Of course not.

You would carefully consider the layout, how it flows, how it feels, and then work backwards to bring it to life. Your life and business deserve the same level of design. When you are clear on your life vision, your business decisions start to make more sense.

You stop chasing what looks good on paper and start building what actually feels good in your day-to-day life.

Goals are milestones. Vision is the destination.

Goals are what you want to achieve. Vision is the life you want to live.

For example, a goal might be: *"Reach $1 million in revenue."*

But a vision sounds more like: *"I want to run a business that gives me the freedom to travel, be present with my family, and make a meaningful impact without burning out."*

Vision gives your goals meaning. It connects your ambition to your purpose.

START WITH YOUR PERSONAL VISION

This comes first, always. Ask yourself: What kind of life do I want to live? This is not just about what you want to do, but how you want to feel. Who you want to be. The rhythm of your days, the energy you bring, the memories you create.

Once you have defined your personal vision, you can shape your business around it. Here is mine, just to spark some ideas:

"I want to live a calm, intentional life, surrounded by family, guided by faith, and filled with freedom and fun. I want a business I can run from anywhere so I can explore the world, powered by a self-led, values-driven team. I want to spend my days creating meaningful work, connecting deeply with others, contributing to a better world, and being a great example for my kids. I love to learn and grow, and share what I learn with others so we can all rise together."

THEN BUILD YOUR BUSINESS VISION

Your business vision is the bridge between your personal vision and your entrepreneurial reality.

It answers the question: What kind of business do I need to build in order to live that life? Ask yourself:

- What kind of business model supports the lifestyle I want?
- How big does it need to be, and what is enough?
- What role do I want to play long term; CEO, visionary, advisor, or eventually none?

- What kind of team and culture would give me peace and freedom?
- Who do I want to serve, and how do I want to impact them?
- What do I want this business to be remembered for?

A powerful business vision is not just about profit, it is about purpose and positioning. It paints a picture of where the company is heading in three to five years. It guides hiring decisions, product innovation, culture, and even exit strategy.

Here is my business vision:

"To build a values-led and profitable company that creates freedom for entrepreneurs by connecting them with world-class remote talent. A business that provides meaningful jobs globally, runs without my daily involvement, and creates space for me to focus on family, travel and other passions."

LESSONS FROM VIVID VISION BY CAMERON HEROLD

One of the best tools I have used for building a clear business vision is Cameron Herold's book *Vivid Vision*. In it, he explains that most entrepreneurs keep their vision too vague, a few bullet points or goals scribbled down. A vivid vision, on the other hand, is a detailed three to five year snapshot of your future company, written as if it already exists.

It is not just numbers on a page. It describes what your culture feels like, what your office or remote team looks like, what the media is writing about you, how your customers describe you, and how you spend your time as the leader.

The lessons that stuck with me were:

- *Write in the present tense.* Describe your company as if you have already achieved it. This tricks your brain into believing and acting as though it is real.
- *Make it visual and emotional.* Do not just talk about revenue, describe how it feels to walk into your business.
- *Share it widely.* A vision only works if your team, investors, and partners can see it and align with it.

When I finished reading the book, I blocked out a day, sat on a hill over-looking the water near my house, and spent time visualising. I felt inspired, motivated and had a deep sense of clarity when I finished. Although the revenue number I wrote down has not yet come to fruition, the way I wanted to run my business has become a reality. That vision gave me a plan to focus on. I also learned to hold the timeline loosely, trusting that everything has its timing.

Below is a short example written for a small but growing business. Notice how it is written in the present tense, as if it has already happened, and focuses not only on numbers but also on culture, clients, systems, and lifestyle.

"It is June 2027 and my business has grown into a small but mighty team of six people. We are a mix of local and remote staff, all aligned by shared values of excellence, kindness, and

accountability. The energy in our meetings is positive and focused. Everyone knows their role, and I no longer feel like I have to carry the business alone.

Our clients describe us as approachable, reliable, and innovative. They love that we go the extra mile and treat their business like our own. Most of our new work now comes from referrals because our clients genuinely enjoy working with us and see the results we deliver.

The brand is becoming known in our niche. We are invited to speak on podcasts, contribute articles, and collaborate with other businesses. We may not be the biggest company, but we are respected for the quality of our work and the authenticity of our approach. The business runs more smoothly because we have systems in place for sales, on-boarding, and delivery. I am no longer doing everything myself. My operations manager keeps projects moving, and my marketing assistant ensures our message is consistently reaching the right people.

I now spend most of my time on the work that excites me: developing new offerings, building relationships with key partners, and mentoring my team.

This allows me to have more free evenings with my family and the flexibility to take short trips without worrying about things falling apart. Most importantly, the business feels aligned with the life I want. It gives me income, impact, and freedom without sacrificing my health, family, or peace of mind."

Now it is your turn. Use the prompts below to write your own vivid vision.

Imagine your business three to five years from now and describe it in the present tense, as if it is already real.

Step 1: Set the Scene (3–5 years from now)

Write the date and describe your company as if it already exists in the future. Be specific, detailed, and present tense.

Step 2: Team and Culture

Describe what it feels like to work in your company. How does your team show up? What is the culture like? How do people feel when they come to work?

Step 3: Clients and Customers

Describe how your customers talk about you, what they experience, and how they feel after working with you.

Step 4: Brand and Recognition

Describe how the outside world sees your business. What are the media, partners, or industry peers saying about you?

Step 5: Operations and Systems

Describe how the business runs day to day. What processes, systems, or leadership make it possible to grow without burning out?

Step 6: Impact and Legacy

Describe the bigger picture of what your business achieves beyond profit. What difference are you making in the world, your industry, or your community?

Step 7: Your Role and Lifestyle

Describe how your role has evolved and how the business supports your ideal life.

FINAL THOUGHTS

You cannot hit a target you have not defined. When your personal and business visions are clear, your strategy becomes a whole lot simpler.

It is no longer just about growth, it is about alignment. And alignment is what brings both peace and performance.

In the next chapter we will explore how to anchor that vision to your values so your daily decisions reflect what you truly stand for.

ACTION STEPS

1. **Write Your Personal Vision Statement**
   Describe your ideal life. Focus on how you want to feel and what you want to experience.
2. **Write Your Business Vision Statement**
   Define what kind of business would best support that life. What do you want it to look like, and what role do you want in it?
3. **Read & Create Your Vivid Vision**
   Read Cameron Herold's book, then find an inspiring location to write a three to five year detailed vivid vision of your business and life.

CHAPTER 2.2

Aligning Your Values with How You Operate

It's one thing to write down what you value. It's another thing entirely to live by it. This chapter is about closing the gap between who you say you are and how you actually show up in your business and life.

When your actions reflect your values, you feel grounded, fulfilled, and proud of how you lead. When they don't, you feel disconnected, anxious, and out of alignment, even if things "look" successful on the outside.

Many entrepreneurs unintentionally build lives that conflict with their core values not because they don't care, but because they've never stopped long enough to check whether their *operations* align with their *beliefs*. Let's make sure you don't build success that silently drains you.

WHAT ARE VALUES, REALLY?

Your values are your personal compass. They guide your decisions, behaviours, and priorities.

Tony Robbins teaches that our values are the emotional states we strive to experience most and they shape every decision we make. The most effective leaders are crystal clear on what they value most and use those values as a compass to guide how they live, lead and build their businesses.

As Tony says, *"Values are like a compass. They give us direction and help us stay on course when the seas of life get stormy."* In short, values are not just beliefs, they're lived behaviours.

At my company Outsourcing Angel, our values are rooted in what I personally believe in and strive to live by. They shape our culture, how we serve our clients, and how we support one another as a team.

Here's what we stand for:

- **Care:** We genuinely care for our clients, our team, and the communities we serve. It's about kindness, empathy, and going the extra mile to make a difference.
- **Courage:** We are bold in the face of challenges. We speak up, take ownership, and embrace discomfort as a path to growth.
- **Innovate:** We don't settle for "how it's always been done." We think differently, stay curious, and continuously find better ways to add value.
- **Integrity:** We do what's right, even when no one's watching. Honesty, accountability, and strong ethics are non-negotiables.

These values aren't just part of our brand, they reflect how I live my life, both in business and beyond. And while these are the values that guide my behaviour, the things I value most in life or the things I protect and prioritise above all are *Faith, Freedom, Fulfilment, Family, and Fun.*

Every decision I make is aligned with those five. I make sure to check in with myself:

1. **Faith:** *Am I living in a way that would please God or am I trying to impress the world?*
2. **Freedom:** *Does this decision create more space and flexibility in my life or does it take it away?*
3. **Fulfilment:** *Does this make me feel deeply purposeful and aligned?*

4. Family: *Is this supporting or stealing from the quality of my family life?*
5. Fun: *Does this bring me joy and make my heart sing?*

These questions help me stay grounded and ensure I'm living in alignment with my most authentic self.

WHERE MISALIGNMENT SHOWS UP

Misalignment is sneaky. You might be doing all the "right" things and still feel wrong inside. Some common signs:

- You say yes when you mean no
- You overwork and justify it as "just a season"
- You feel guilty resting or taking time off
- You build offers, teams, or structures that don't actually feel good
- You make decisions from fear or approval-seeking instead of values

Stephen Covey, author of The 7 Habits of Highly Effective People, says:

"You have to decide what your highest priorities are and have the courage—pleasantly, smilingly, non-apologetically to say 'no' to other things. And the way you do that is by having a bigger 'yes' burning inside."

When you don't know what your "bigger yes" is, everything else runs the show.

I remember during a challenging season in the business, an ex-business partner said to me, *"Why don't we just put everyone in an office so we can control them more?"* We were facing some operational issues at the time, and he believed that having everyone in one physical space would solve the problem.

But my answer was clear: *"Absolutely not."*

I didn't leave the corporate world to recreate it. I built this business for freedom, to be present with my family, to work from anywhere, and to give others that same opportunity. Why would I strip away the very thing that inspired me to start in the first place?

I stayed true to my value of *freedom*.

That's why Outsourcing Angel has always been fully remote.

And despite the challenges, we found better solutions, not by controlling people, but by trusting them, empowering them, and improving our systems.

Since he left, we've doubled the business. More importantly, we've created a culture where people genuinely appreciate the freedom they have to work from home and design a life that works for them. Because when you lead with your values, you don't just build a business. You build a way of life.

THANKYOU – BUILDING A BUSINESS AROUND VALUES

One of the best examples of values-aligned business in Australia is Thankyou, the social enterprise co-founded by Daniel Flynn. From the beginning, their mission was crystal clear:

To help end global poverty by funding life-changing projects through everyday consumer spending.

Rather than prioritising profits, Thankyou chose to direct 100% of their profits to impactful causes and they've given over $17 million to date. But it's not just what they give, it's *how* they operate. In 2020, they famously turned down offers from two of Australia's largest supermarkets when the terms didn't align with their purpose-led mission.

Instead, they launched a bold campaign called "No Small Plan" to seek global partnerships that shared their values. They've also remained radically transparent, publishing detailed reports and maintaining high levels of integrity across their operations.

This example shows that you don't have to compromise values for growth. You can be profitable and principled.

Their story proves that people are drawn to authenticity, and that standing firm in your values even when it's difficult can actually fuel your success.

FINAL THOUGHTS

So what does this mean for you? It means your personal values matter not just in theory, but in practice. When you're clear on what truly matters to you, you make better decisions.

You attract the right people.
You build a life and business that feels aligned, not forced.

Because at the end of the day, success is not just about what you build. It's about who you become while building it. So take the time to define your values. Write them down. Check in with them often. Let them guide how you show up in your leadership, your relationships, your decisions, and your everyday life.

That's how you create a life and business you're truly proud of. This is what 360° Success is all about: Building a business and life that feels right, not just looks good.

ACTION STEPS

1. **Identify Your Core Values**
   Write down 10 values that matter to you. Circle your top 3–5 that feel non-negotiable.
2. **Audit for Alignment**
   Take a look at how you're spending your time, running your business, and making decisions. What's aligned and what isn't?
3. **Choose One Shift**
   Pick one misaligned area and make a small change today that brings you closer to living your values.

CHAPTER 2.3

Clarifying Goals That Actually Matter

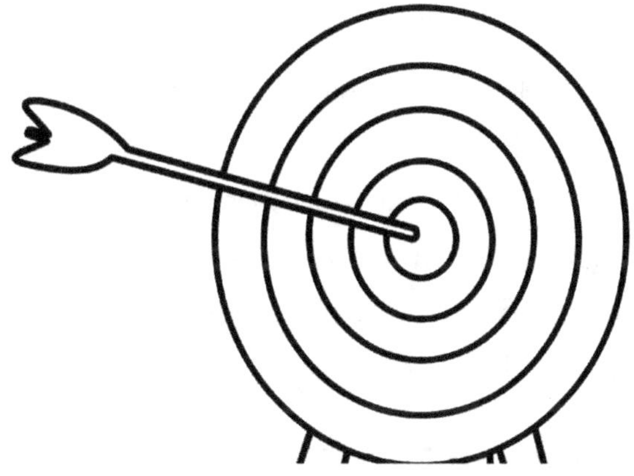

You've probably set a lot of goals in your life. Revenue targets. Growth milestones. New habits. A million to-do lists. But how many of those goals actually moved the needle on your happiness, your fulfilment, or your freedom?

Setting goals is easy. Setting goals that actually matter... that's where most people get stuck. In this chapter, we'll strip away the noise and help you set goals that align with your values, serve your vision, and support your journey toward 360° Success.

THE PROBLEM WITH TRADITIONAL GOAL-SETTING

Traditional goal-setting is often:

- Driven by ego or comparison
- Focused only on external metrics (money, scale, status)
- Disconnected from values or purpose
- Outcome-obsessed, with no real attention on how it feels to pursue or achieve them

This leads to what I call hollow wins; goals you hit that leave you asking, *"Is this all there is?"*

A study in Harvard Business Review found that people are 42% more likely to achieve their goals when they write them down but even more important than writing them is choosing goals that are emotionally meaningful. Because without meaning, a goal is just another task. With meaning, it becomes a milestone in your personal transformation.

WHAT DO MEANINGFUL GOALS LOOK LIKE?

Meaningful goals are anchored in clarity. They support the kind of life and business you actually want to live not the version that looks good to your peers or online audience.

They don't just make your business better. They make you better. Let's say:

- **You value freedom** - A meaningful goal might be: *"Reduce my involvement in daily operations to under 10 hours/week."*

- You value family - *"Have one uninterrupted family dinner each night and take a 2-week unplugged holiday this year."*
- You value faith - *"Start each day with 30 minutes of prayer and journalling."*
- You value growth - *"Read one book per month and attend a transformational retreat this year."*

Now compare that to generic goals like:

"Make $2M this year."
"Get 100k followers."
"Win 5 awards."

There's nothing wrong with those goals but if they're not connected to what you truly value, they can leave you feeling empty, even when you hit them.

I've been guilty of this too. I used to let other people's idea of success get in my head. Sometimes I was just too lazy to stop and think about what I actually wanted.

I let status and validation run me. I'd see someone else's highlight reel and think, *"If they can do it, so can I."*

But every time I chased someone else's version of success, my happiness took a hit.

GOAL EXAMPLES FOR EACH OF THE 5 PILLARS

Let's bring the concept of values-aligned goals into focus by looking at the 5 Pillars of 360° Success. Instead of setting 25 scattered goals, I encourage you to start with just one meaningful goal per pillar. This creates clarity, focus, and momentum without the overwhelm. First, a quick reminder of the 5 Pillars:

1. **Empowered Connection:** Friends, colleagues, business network, community, contribution.
2. **Business Freedom:** Time and financial independence
3. **Self-Mastery:** Body, mind, and soul
4. **Family Balance:** Partner, kids, and extended family
5. **Life Experiences:** Adventure, travel, hobbies, joy

You've probably heard of SMART goals:

Specific, Measurable, Achievable, Relevant, and Time-bound. But I want to evolve that concept with something more powerful: SMART+H, where the H stands for Heart.

It's not enough for your goals to make logical sense. They need to mean something emotionally. That's what keeps you committed when motivation fades.

For example: *"Increase profit by 20%"* vs. *"Increase profit by 20% so I can fund a family sabbatical and hire support to free up my time."* One is a goal. The other is a *mission* with heart.

SMART+H GOAL EXAMPLES FOR EACH PILLAR

Here are some examples to inspire you:

1. Empowered Connection

"Reach out intentionally to one person each weekday whether it's a friend, team member, or someone in my network for the next 90 days. It could be a message of appreciation, encouragement, or simply checking in."

2. Business Freedom

"Reduce my operational involvement to under 10 hours per week within 6 months by hiring a general manager so I can focus on strategy and enjoy more space in my life."

3. Self-Mastery

"Commit to a consistent fitness routine by doing three strength workouts, two online work-outs and two walks per week for the next 12 weeks so I can improve my energy, mental clarity, and show up as my best self."

4. Family Balance

"Block out school pickup and family dinner time from 4:30 to 7:30pm every weekday for the next 90 days so I can reconnect daily and be fully present with my kids."

5. Life Experiences

"Book a two-week overseas family holiday within the next three months and unplug from work completely so I can create unforgettable memories and recharge fully."

A PERSONAL EXAMPLE

In the past, one of my goals was simply to "scale my business." On the surface, it sounded right. But when I got honest with myself, what I really wanted was:

- To free myself from day-to-day operations
- To empower my team to lead
- To work less and spend more quality time with my family

So I re-framed the goal into something aligned with my values: "Redesign the business to run without me in daily ops so I can work under 20 hours per week and still hit our revenue targets."

That one shift changed everything. It aligned my time, energy, and purpose and ultimately, brought me peace.

FINAL THOUGHTS

You don't need more goals, you need the right goals. The ones that:

- Reflect who you're becoming
- Honour your values and vision
- Serve your life not just your bottom line

Because when your goals are in harmony with your identity and purpose, you'll not only achieve them, you'll enjoy the journey of becoming the person who lives them out. And isn't that what we're really chasing?

In the next chapter, we will turn goals into practical action steps, starting with designing your year. Too many people drift through the year hoping things will improve, hoping for more time, more balance, more fulfilment, without ever pausing to design it. This chapter is about shifting from wishful thinking to intentional action.

This is where the real momentum begins.

ACTION STEPS

1. **Review Your Vision & Values**
   Revisit Chapters 2.1 and 2.2 to reconnect with what matters most to you right now.
2. **Set One Goal for Each of the 5 Pillars using the SMART+H Framework**
   Ask yourself: "What is one aligned goal in each area that would shift how I live and lead?"
3. **Choose Your Focus**
   You don't need to do it all at once. Pick 1–2 to focus on over the next 90 days.

Section 3. Designing Your Life & Business with Intention

"You can't hit a target you can't see, and you can't live a life you haven't designed." — Jim Rohn

CHAPTER 3.1

Mapping Out Your Ideal Year

We're all familiar with the idea of goal-setting and resolutions at the start of a year. But let's be honest, many of those goals don't make it past February.

Why? Because most people set goals, but they don't design their year to support those goals. They plan projects, launches, and to-do lists but they forget to intentionally map out what matters most: their people, their joy, and their *life.*

This chapter is about flipping the script. Instead of life reacting to your business, your business should be designed to support your *life.*

Years ago, I was sitting in a life coaching session with Uma when she asked me something I'll never forget:

"What does success look like for you as a mum? As a wife? As a leader?"

As I reflected, I realised my definition of success was tied to who I needed to be and what I needed to do in each role. For me, it looked like:

- Taking my kids on holiday twice a year to feel connected
- Going on monthly date nights with my husband to nurture our relationship
- Having quiet mornings to journal, pray, and centre myself
- Take my team on an annual company trip to bond and grow together

And then it hit me: success isn't an accident. It's the result of intentional planning.

WHY ANNUAL PLANNING MATTERS

Without a clear vision for your year, your calendar fills up with what's urgent, not what's truly important.

As an exercise, Uma asked me to pull out an excel sheet with a calendar template and start blocking out time for the things that matter. So I opened up the sheet and began entering dates for family birthdays, school holidays, and weekends away with friends.

That one exercise changed how I lived my life forever. It's the foundation of 360° Success: designing your life around your values and intentionally decide who and when you want to spend time with.

And here's the golden rule I now live by: *Plan life first. Business second.* That means pro-actively locking in what matters to your heart before you start filling in meetings, launches, and business goals. Start with:

- Family commitments like birthdays, anniversaries, school holidays, church services
- Date nights and weekend getaways
- Vacations (even if you don't know where you'll go yet, just block the time)

When something involves others, like my husband, I don't wait until I've figured it all out. I just send him a "Save the Date" calendar invite and protect the time. Details can come later. But if you don't lock it in, life gets crowded and the moments that matter slip through the cracks.

I started with a simple Excel spreadsheet, colour coding each category: husband, kids, friends and business. It gave me a clean visual of the year, month by month of how I'm dedicating time to the important areas of my life.

Now I use Notion, where I've created a digital life planning hub and share it with my team or family, and easily adjust as life evolves.

Whether you use a paper planner, Excel, Notion, or Google Calendar, what matters is doing it with intention. The tool is less important than the mindset behind it.

VISUAL EXAMPLE: A SIMPLE IDEAL YEAR LAYOUT

Month	Key Focus/Theme	Life Pillars Mapped
January	Planning & Recovery	Company Retreat , school holidays, quality time with kids
February	Launch Prep	Team strategy session, date night
March	Launch	Business sprint, kids' birthday weekend
April	Family & Fun	School holidays, short getaway
May	Self-Mastery	Health reset, couple's retreat
June	Mid-Year Review	Vision planning, girls' trip, family dinner
July	Rest & Travel	Overseas family holiday (2 weeks)
August	Creation & Vision	Content retreat, no meetings week
September	Growth	Mastermind event, business conference

October	Family Focus	Kids' school events, weekend unplugged trip
November	Wind Down	Wrap up key goals, simplify schedule
December	Reflection & Joy	Christmas, family traditions, sabbatical time

This is just a sample to get your creativity flowing. Your year will look different depending on your life season, your energy rhythms, and your business needs.

FINAL THOUGHTS

Mapping your year doesn't mean locking yourself into a rigid plan. It means claiming space for what matters. It means becoming the kind of person who doesn't just hope for a great year but designs it with intention.

Because your life isn't something you squeeze into the cracks of your business. It's the reason you're building your business.

In the next chapter, we'll zoom in and explore how to design your ideal day because your best year is really just a series of well-lived days.

Let's keep going.

ACTION STEPS

1. **Download or print a Year-at-a-Glance Calendar**
   Or use your favourite digital planning tool (Notion, Google Calendar, Excel)
2. **Block in your personal non-negotiables first**
   (Vacations, birthdays, holidays, retreats, family events)
3. **Add a "Save the Date" invite for any plans that involve others** (Even if you haven't figured out all the details yet!)
4. **Design your business plans around your life**
   Add launch periods, planning weeks, team events after your personal pillars are protected
5. **Create a one-word theme for the year or quarterly themes to keep you inspired**
   E.g. Strategic/ Build / Simplify / Celebrate
6. **Share your calendar with your team or family**
   So they can support and honour your intentions

CHAPTER 3.2

Designing Your Ideal Day

They say how you spend your days is how you spend your life and I believe that's true.

We often think success is built in the big moments: launches, awards, milestones. But real success? It's found in the ordinary. In the small decisions. In how you show up each day. That's why designing your ideal day matters. Because if you don't intentionally shape it, your day will be ruled by distractions, reactivity, and exhaustion. And when your days feel off, life feels off.

This chapter is about helping you reclaim your time not by doing more, but by structuring your day with purpose so your energy goes where it matters most.

HOW WAKING UP EARLY CHANGED EVERYTHING

I've always admired people who could wake up early. You know the type, those 4am CEOs and high performers who say things like *"I've done more before 7am than most do all day."* They always seemed like another species. *Disciplined. Focused. Energised.* And I wondered, how do they do it?

Some of the world's most successful people swear by early mornings:

- Apple CEO Tim Cook wakes at 3:45am to work out and start emails early.
- Mark Wahlberg famously begins his day at 2:30am, fitting in a workout, prayer, and family time *before* 7am.
- Oprah Winfrey starts her day around 6am with meditation, reading, and walking.

I admired these people and knew that if I had more time, I could do more too. But deep down, I didn't believe I was one of those people. That all changed during a holiday in Vietnam with my assistant Wendy in 2016. One morning, I woke up at 8am and there she was, already beaming with a big smile.

"What would you like for breakfast, Ms Linh?" She asked in her sweet and energetic Filipino accent. I was stunned by how alive and refreshed she looked so early in the day. When I asked where all that energy came from, she simply said *"I've been up since 4am. I always wake up early. It gives me time for myself."*

That was the spark. If Wendy could do it, so could I. Seeing a real life example, gave me the confidence I needed to believe in myself.

Nowadays, I go to bed by 9pm and wake up at 3am. But it didn't start that way. It was a gradual shift. I began by waking up at 5am for a while, then practised 4am, and eventually settled into 3am after four years of consistent early rising.

And then I discovered something magical. Waking up early didn't just give me more time. I discovered that I was the smartest, most productive, most creative version of myself in the early morning, when I'm fully recharged after a good night's sleep. I became hooked on the results I could create in that quiet, sacred window of the day. It gave me space to do the things that truly fill my soul.

I start with gratitude journalling, set my intentions for the day, write through whatever challenges are on my mind, and pray to God for guidance. I also use this time for high impact work, the kind that requires deep thinking, focus, and creativity. Whether it's writing, planning, content creation, or making important business decisions, this is when I do my best thinking. I bond with my husband over a quick coffee before he heads to work. By 6:30am, I already feel productive and my soul is satisfied. Then I head to the gym, free from distractions.

These days, I can actually feel the difference when I sleep in. On mornings I wake later than usual, I notice my mood shifts. I feel more sluggish, grumpier, and less motivated. That's why keeping this habit is easier. It simply makes me happier.

Now, you're probably wondering, do I ever go out? Of course I do. If I have an event or a late night, I don't force myself to get up at 3am the next morning. Instead, I make sure I get a full six hours of sleep and wake a little later. I never compromise on rest.

Sleep isn't optional, it's foundational.

And here's something interesting I've learned along the way. The quality of your sleep matters more than the number of hours.

Research from places like Harvard Medical School and the Sleep Foundation shows that consistent sleep routines, going to bed and waking up at the same time every day, play a bigger role in your energy, focus, and well being than just getting more hours here and there. In short, your routine shapes the quality of your rest.

If there's one habit that makes every other habit easier, it's waking up early. Most people know they should meditate, journal, exercise, or plan their day, but they don't feel they have time. They prioritise sleeping in, and as a result, they miss the window to fit those life changing habits in. Then they wake up feeling behind and spend the rest of the day reacting to whatever life throws at them. I highly recommend challenging yourself to wake up a little earlier each day and see how your life begins to shift, just like mine did.

DESIGNING YOUR IDEAL DAY

Designing your ideal day doesn't mean every minute is rigidly scheduled. It's about setting a clear intention for how to optimise your time so it doesn't slip away unnoticed.

Too often, the day begins in reaction mode, waking up to your phone, scrolling through feeds, and filling your mind with noise before you've even started. Instead, create a rhythm that works with your energy, not against it. That means tackling high-energy, creative work earlier in the day and leaving lighter tasks for later.

Here's a framework you can use to design your day with intention:

1. Morning Ritual (Your Inner World)
    - Prayer, journalling, reading
    - Meditation or breathwork
    - Set your top 3 intentions for the day
2. Focus Time (Your Deep Work)
    - Block time for strategy, creation, delivery
    - Mute notifications, turn off distractions
3. Connection Time (Your People)
    - Family meals, school runs, coffee with friends

- Evening tech-free zones with your partner or kids

4. Admin / Light Tasks (Your Maintenance)

- Schedule lighter tasks later in the day for when your energy dips
- Delegate where possible

5. Evening Routine (Your Wind Down)

- Gratitude journalling or reflections
- No screens an hour before bed
- Light reading or quality time with family before bed

Here's what a typical day looks like for me:

Time	Activity
3:00am	Wake up
3:30–4:00am	Journalling, prayer, meditation
4:00–5:30am	Focussed creative work (writing, strategy, vision)
5:30–6:00am	Coffee time with my husband
6:00–7:00am	Workout or walk
7:00–9:00am	Kids' morning routine and school prep
9:30am–3:00pm	Work (calls, meetings, focused tasks)
3:30pm onward	Kids & family time
9:00pm	Sleep

This rhythm allows me to fill my own cup first so I can give to my family, team, and clients from a place of calm and purpose, not chaos and depletion.

HOW ALCOHOL KEPT ME FROM LIVING MY IDEAL DAY

There was one thing that kept getting in the way of my habit of waking up early and following my ideal day. It was alcohol. No matter how well I planned, drinking would undo it all. I would stay up too late, sleep poorly, and the next day I would feel sluggish, unmotivated, and even depressed. I would miss my morning routine, skip the gym, and spend the day just trying to catch up. And when I did wake up, it often came with shame, guilt, and regret.

I tried quitting once. I stopped drinking for eight months and felt amazing. Clear headed, consistent, and focused. But then I thought I could come back and drink in moderation. Just a wine here and there. But it never stayed that way. One drink turned into two, and before I knew it, I was back where I started.

Trust me, I made all sorts of rules for myself. Only one glass at functions. A maximum of three on special occasions. Only drink on birthdays. Stick to wine, no spirits. Whatever the rule was, it never worked. I would always find a way to drink more than I should. I went out more than I needed to. I got easily persuaded by friends. And once I was in the middle of the fun, all my logic went out the window.

Alcohol is sneaky like that. It makes you lose control, wastes your time, and pulls you further away from the life you are trying to build. And let's be real, hangovers hit harder when you are older.

I was tired of the mental fog, the wasted mornings, and the constant cycle of starting over. Like many others, I told myself I was not addicted. I did not drink every day. I was not an alcoholic. But once I actually tried to quit, I realised how deeply alcohol had a grip on me. The truth hit hard. I could not imagine my life without it. That is when I knew I had been more dependent than I ever admitted.

On 2 April 2023, after one too many nights of drinking, doing embarrassing things, and losing my phone again, I reached a breaking point.

I remember the exact date so clearly because it marks one of the proudest moments of my life. It was the day I finally walked away from alcohol for good. Why? Because I changed a part of myself I thought was permanent. I had always been known as the party girl. The crazy one. The fun, wild one who drank the most, danced the hardest, and never said no to a night out. It was the identity I had carried for as long as I could remember.

Letting that go felt like shedding old skin. Scary at first, but unbelievably freeing. Now that I have been sober for more than 3 years, I realised something powerful. I do not have to put up with hangovers or feeling like crap anymore. It doesn't have to be part of my life. I do not have to keep pressing reset on my goals. I can choose to redesign my life without alcohol and still have fun. I did not lose anything. I gained clarity, energy, and peace. I can actually follow through on my ideal day.

Some of my newer friends assumed I quit easily. They thought I was superwoman, being able to walk away from alcohol just like that. What they did not realise is that I started drinking when I was 16, and I had wanted to quit for nearly three decades. It was hard. Probably the hardest thing I have ever done. But I am here to tell you that if I can do it, so can you.

I am grateful that my journey has also inspired some of my fellow entrepreneurs to quit drinking. Watching them become happier and more present makes every part of my sobriety worth it. They are also part of the reason I won't give up. I want to be a beacon of hope for anyone battling addiction and longing for a better life. By connecting my choice to something bigger than myself, I've been able to stay strong.

Quitting alcohol was not about giving something up. It was about finally choosing the life I was meant to live. I have saved so much time, money, and emotional energy. I no longer carry that guilt. I laugh more. I show up fully. And most importantly, I am proud of the example I am setting for my kids.

FINAL THOUGHTS

You don't need to be Mark Wahlberg or Oprah. But you do need to decide what kind of person you want to become and design a day that supports that version of you.

Do you want to be a good example to your children?
Do you want to be the best leader for your team?
Do you want to inspire others through your actions?

Then ask yourself: what can you do each day to support that? And just as importantly, what habits are holding you back from living your ideal day? Even one small change like waking up an hour earlier or carving out time to practise gratitude can transform how you lead, live, and love. The key is consistency.

Just like babies thrive on routines, so do we. A steady rhythm leads to better sleep, more energy, and a stronger foundation for everything else in life. Your ideal life doesn't begin with a perfect schedule. It begins with one intentional day and the courage to repeat it.

In Chapter 7.4, we'll dive deeper into making habits stick and how to stay consistent with anything you put your mind to. But first, in the next chapter, we'll explore how to set boundaries so your ideal day doesn't get hijacked by guilt, distractions, or overcommitment.

ACTION STEPS

1. **Define your Ideal Wake + Sleep Times**
   What time do you want to go to sleep and wake up to feel your best?
2. **Sketch Your Ideal Day**
   Include: Morning rituals, focus work, family time, rest, connection, and joy
3. **Pick 3 Daily Non-Negotiables**
   These are your soul anchors, protect them fiercely
4. **Try One Change This Week**
   Start small: wake 30 mins earlier, turn off screens by 8pm, add a morning walk

CHAPTER 3.3

Setting Boundaries That Protect Your Peace

If you're constantly overwhelmed, overstretched, or over-committed, chances are, you don't have a time problem. You have a *boundary* problem. Boundaries aren't about building walls. They're about creating *rhythms* that protect your time, energy, and peace so you can focus on the things that truly matter.

As entrepreneurs, we often take pride in being flexible and saying yes to everything. But without boundaries, that flexibility becomes a trap. You lose yourself trying to be everything to everyone. And soon enough, your time belongs to your inbox, your to-do list, and everyone else's priorities but not to you.

IF YOU DON'T FILL YOUR CALENDAR, SOMEONE ELSE WILL

Here's a simple but powerful truth: *When you fill your calendar with the things that matter, you leave less space for the things that don't.*

So often I hear people say, *"I just don't have time."*

But the truth is, it's rarely a lack of time, it's how we're using it. Hours get swallowed by scrolling, TV, or other distractions, and we mistake busyness for productivity.

I learned this lesson first-hand when I took on the 75 Hard Challenge, a couple of years ago. *75 Hard Challenge* isn't just a fitness challenge, it's a mental toughness and habit-building program created by Andy Frisella. For 75 days straight, I had to:

- Do two 45-minute workouts daily (one outdoors)
- Drink 4 litres of water
- Read 10 pages of a personal development book
- Follow a strict diet (no alcohol, no cheat meals)
- Take a daily progress photo

This challenge was brutal, but it was also incredibly *rewarding*. I remember going for walks at 8 p.m. in the rain, running laps around the airport car park, and reading late at night after going to an event. Yet every time I ticked the check-box for the day, I felt proud of what I'd achieved. I became more focused, determined, and disciplined. My kids were amazed and sometimes even joined in on the fun.

What I discovered was that because my schedule was already filled with productive habits, I simply didn't have time for mindless scrolling or TV binges. The challenge proved that we can always make time if we really want to. Yes, it's extreme, but doing it once was enough to show me the truth about priorities and the power of boundaries.

I highly recommend trying this challenge at least once in your life, not just for physical reasons (I did lose a few kgs), but because it's an incredible way to build resilience and discipline. You'll be amazed at what happens when you stop leaving your day up to chance.

That's why I'm such a big believer in calendar planning. When you map out the non-negotiables, your rest time, family time, holidays, even fun, you're not limiting yourself... You're liberating yourself. You're making a statement: *This is what matters. Everything else can wait.*

For me personally, I used to think setting boundaries meant being selfish. I was scared to say no. I didn't want to let anyone down. I said yes out of guilt, not alignment.

But over time, I realised something: The more I said yes to others, the more I was saying no to myself.

No to rest.
No to my kids.
No to my health.
No to my peace.

I was working more, achieving more... but *feeling* less. Less connected. Less calm. Less like me. Eventually, I realised something important: *Boundaries don't restrict your life, they protect your peace.* And peace is priceless.

I want to be real with you, I don't always stick to my boundaries perfectly. Sometimes life gets busy. Sometimes I get caught in the "just one more meeting" spiral. Sometimes I say yes out of habit or excitement. I fall off the boundary wagon. But the difference now is I catch it quickly.

I've trained myself to notice when I've crossed a line. My body feels more tired. My joy dips. My family gets less of me. That's my cue to reset.

So if you mess up, it doesn't mean you're failing. It just means you're human. Boundaries aren't about perfection. They're about coming back again and again, to the life you *actually* want.

MY BOUNDARY SUPERPOWER

One of the best things I ever did to support my boundaries was hiring my incredible virtual assistant, Seeta.

I made a commitment to not work during school holidays so I can be fully present with my kids. But as we all know, the world doesn't stop just because you want it to. Seeta helps me hold the line.

She blocks off my calendar, declines meeting requests, and even reminds *me* not to say yes when I'm tempted to squeeze something in. Having someone in your corner who respects your time as much as you do is a game changer. If you struggle to uphold your boundaries, don't just rely on willpower, build in support.

TRY A MAYBE/NOT NOW LIST

Here's a little hack that changed everything for me. If something is a *Hell Yes!*, I add it to my to-do list and say yes straight away to whoever has asked me.

If it's not a *Hell Yes!*, I place it into one of two lists:

- *Maybe List* – These are opportunities or ideas I genuinely like and may want to go ahead with but I need a little more time, clarity, or information before committing.
- *Not Now List* – Ideas I like but don't want to think about right now. These get parked for the future, so I can revisit them when the timing is right.

Now, when someone asks me to speak at an event, join a group, or start a new project, I simply say: *"Let me get back to you next week."* I forward the request to my assistant for her to do due diligence and to see if it matches my priorities and values.

I also allow time to do the filtering, if after a while my heart feels called to do something then I would. This process has helped me avoid saying yes too soon, stay in integrity with my real priorities, and keep my life feeling peaceful and spacious.

EXAMPLES OF BOUNDARIES

One of the most inspiring boundary rituals I've come across comes from my interview with Rabbi Daniel Lapin. He spoke about the Jewish tradition of observing the Sabbath, an entire day set aside for rest, worship, and connection.

It's not a "maybe if there's time" day. It's sacred. It's planned. And it's protected.

Phones are off. Business is paused. Families gather. Reflection happens. Joy is prioritised. It's such a beautiful example of what boundaries can look like when they're rooted in love, not restriction, and embraced by the whole family.

Other boundary role models include:

- Warren Buffett who famously protects his time with an empty calendar. He says the secret to success is learning to say "no" to almost everything.
- Arianna Huffington built a company around hustle until she collapsed from burnout. Now, she's an advocate for strong boundaries around sleep, tech, and well-being.
- Michelle Obama said she used to wake up at 4:30am to work out, not because it was easy, but because it was the only time she had for herself. She protected that space because it gave her the energy to show up for everyone else.

These leaders don't apologise for their boundaries. And neither should you.

Below are the simple boundaries I've made for myself:

1. **3–6am is mine:** Prayer, journalling, strategic thinking, and deep work. No messages. No noise. Just alignment.
2. **No meetings after 3pm:** So I can spend quality time with my kids or attend an event that matters to me.
3. **Evening wind down by 8pm:** No late night calls or commitments. No phones before bed.
4. **School holidays off:** No work. No meetings. Just time with kids.

FINAL THOUGHTS

Your time is your life. Your boundaries are how you protect it. You won't always get it right and that's okay. What matters most is that you're aware, intentional, and willing to come back to what matters when you drift.

Let your calendar reflect your values.
Let your no be a gift to your future self.

And let your boundaries become the quiet structure that supports your freedom. When you honour your limits, you create space for what really matters: peace, connection, energy, and joy.

In the next chapter, we'll talk about making space for what fuels you because boundaries aren't just about saying no. They're about saying yes to the life you were made for.

ACTION STEPS

1. **Audit Your Energy Leaks**
   Where are you saying yes when you actually mean no?
2. **Try the 75 Hard Challenge**
   Or create your own version. Fill your time with discipline, and watch the noise fade.
3. **Create Your Yes & Maybe Lists**
   Review your Maybes fortnightly or monthly. Say yes only to what aligns.
4. **Enlist Support**
   Ask your VA or team to help protect your non-negotiables.
5. **Add a Weekly Sabbath**
   Even half a day. No work. No screens. Just rest, reflection, and reconnection.

CHAPTER 3.4

Creating Space for What Fuels You

By now, you've learned how to map your whole year, design your ideal day and build boundaries around what matters. But creating space isn't just about scheduling, it's about believing that you're allowed to pause.

And it's also about seeing how space isn't a disruption to success, it's the very thing that makes it possible. If you want to live a full life, you have to stop filling every moment.

This chapter is all about helping you create intentional space for your five pillars not just on paper, but in practice.

WHY WE AVOID THE VERY THINGS THAT FUEL US

Let's be honest. We already *know* what fuels us: rest, family, play, meditation, nature, joy. So why is it so hard to make time for it?

1. **Guilt**
   "If I'm not working, I'm being selfish or lazy."
   We've been conditioned to believe rest is earned. But rest is a requirement, not a reward.
2. **Fear of Slowing Down**
   "What if I lose momentum?"
   Especially for entrepreneurs, rest can feel risky like if you pause, you'll fall behind. But it's in the stillness that clarity comes.
3. **Control**
   "If I step away, things might fall apart."
   But stepping away is exactly how you learn where things fall apart so you can build a stronger business and team.

REFRAMING REST AS A STRATEGIC MOVE

Rest is not a sign of weakness. It's a leadership move. At Outsourcing Angel, I introduced a monthly Compulsory Rested Day Off (RDO) for our team.

Everyone gets one long weekend each month: no work and no checking in. But here's the catch: If they don't take the day, they lose it!

This one change not only improved well-being and morale, it built a culture that values balance, not burnout. Everyone looks forward to it. Everyone takes it. Because we treat rest as essential, not optional. And this applies to entrepreneurs too.

A SELF-CARE CHALLENGE FOR HIGH PERFORMERS

If you're someone who struggles to take time off, let me offer you a challenge. Over the next three months, gradually build the habit of rest so it starts to feel *normal* rather than indulgent:

- Month 1: Take half a day off every fortnight
- Month 2: Take half a day off weekly
- Month 3: Take one full day off weekly

In his book *Shine*, Gino Wickman, founder of the Entrepreneurial Operating System (EOS), talks about how he takes a full month off every year as a sabbatical. When I heard that, I thought, wow... a whole month.

I actually did take a month off recently when I travelled through Europe with my family, and it really did feel like a long break. I felt completely detached from work and fully present in life. But to be honest, I've always found one or two weeks away regularly throughout the year to be a good pace for me. Aiming for a full month every year still feels like a stretch, something I'm not totally used to yet.

But hey, if Gino is throwing down the challenge, why not give it a go. It's not really about the time off itself. It's about retraining your nervous system to feel safe letting go. It's about proving to yourself that the business won't crumble if you're not there, and that when you come back, you'll be clearer, calmer and more creative.

And it doesn't have to be all or nothing. Even going from three days off to five, or from one week to two, is progress. Every step we take towards more rest is a win, and each time we do it, we build more trust in ourselves and in our business.

THE POWER OF PERSPECTIVE

Here's the magic no one talks about: *When you take time away, you actually see your business more clearly.*

You'll notice:

- Where your team needs more support
- Which processes are too dependent on you
- What you've been avoiding or over-controlling
- Which team members step up (or don't)

Time off reveals gaps but also unlocks growth. It gives others the chance to lead. It helps you become the *visionary,* not the firefighter. And more importantly, it brings you back to yourself.

MICRO-SPACE VS. MACRO-SPACE

You don't need a month-long sabbatical to start recharging. Rest and renewal can happen in both macro and micro ways and the magic is in building them into your life *consistently.* Think in terms of:

- **Macro-Space:** extended time away to reset, reflect, and reconnect (e.g. week-long holidays, monthly long weekends, spiritual retreats, family getaways)
- **Micro-Space:** small, intentional pauses woven into your everyday routine (e.g. 20 minutes tech-free outdoors, silent coffee before the world wakes up, morning prayer, journalling, afternoon cuddle time with your kids)

Don't underestimate the power of micro-moments. They act like mini resets for your nervous system, giving your mind and body permission to slow down even just for a few minutes.

They remind you that rest isn't something you earn, it's something you need in order to show up as your best self.

WHAT FUELS YOU?

We often say, *"I just need a break,"* but when that rare pocket of free time appears... we freeze. We scroll, we clean, we catch up on errands but we don't actually recharge. Why? Because we haven't defined what rest looks like for us.

Start here: Make your own *Fuel List:* a simple, powerful tool to reconnect with what truly fills your cup. Write down 10 things that genuinely recharge or delight you. Not what *should* relax you, or what looks good on Instagram but the things that make you feel alive, peaceful, or deeply content.

Here are some ideas to get you started:

- A massage
- Walking without your phone
- Reading a book
- Napping without guilt
- Morning coffee alone
- Listening to relaxing music
- Girls' night
- Beach days
- A hot bath with no interruptions
- Journalling in a cosy corner

Keep this list somewhere visible like on your fridge, in your planner, or as a phone screensaver. When you feel drained, anxious, or uninspired, don't push through.

Choose something from the list. Treat it like a menu for your soul, because rest shouldn't be a reward, it should be a rhythm.

UPGRADE YOUR INNER DIALOGUE

Most resistance to rest isn't about logistics, it's about *mindset.* The real challenge is the voice in your head that says:

"There's too much to do."

"Everything will fall apart if you slow down."

That voice is not the truth, it's just an old story. And if you want to lead a more balanced, fulfilling life, it's time to rewrite that narrative.

Here's a new script, one that supports your well-being and your growth:

"Rest is productive."

Because it restores clarity, energy, and perspective; three things every great leader needs.

"I lead better when I'm well."

Your health isn't a luxury. It's a leadership responsibility.

"Fun is fuel, not fluff."

Joy doesn't make you less serious, it makes you more sustainable.

"My team grows when I step back."

Letting go creates space for others to rise.

"I give myself permission to pause even when things aren't perfect."

Because waiting for everything to be done is a trap. There will always be more to do.

Say these out loud. Write them down. Post them on your desk, your mirror, or your phone wallpaper. Let these new truths become the foundation for how you lead, not just in your business, but in your life.

Because your inner dialogue becomes your reality. And if you want a life filled with peace, presence, and purpose, it starts with the words you speak to yourself.

ACTION STEPS

1. **Make Your "Fuel List"**
   Write down 10 activities that genuinely recharge you. Keep it visible and revisit it weekly.
2. **Schedule Micro and Macro Space**
   Add small daily moments (15–30 mins) and bigger breaks (1 day/month or quarterly getaway) to your calendar.
3. **Weekly 5 Pillar Check-In**
   Each Sunday, reflect: Which pillar did I nourish this week? Which one needs more love next week?

CHAPTER 3.5

Creating Your Bucket List

"Fill your life with adventures, not regrets. Have stories to tell, not stuff to show." – Unknown

Have you ever paused long enough to wonder, *"Am I really living or just existing?"* It's so easy to let life slip away without noticing. One week bleeds into the next. Responsibilities pile up. We chase goals, put out fires, and delay joy. We tell ourselves we'll get to it *someday.*

But someday isn't a date on the calendar. And sadly, many people reach the end of their life realising they were too busy to *actually live.* We don't get to choose *how long we live.* But we can choose *how well we live.*

MY BUCKET LIST

In 2010, I discovered the idea of a bucket list, a list of things you want to do before you die. But instead of scribbling it on paper, I opened up an Excel spreadsheet and began typing 100 things I wanted to experience. Some were bold:

✓ Marry the love of my life

✓ Have a baby girl

✓ Go skydiving

✓ Buy my parents a car

Others were simple joys:

✓ Watch the sunrise on a beach

✓ Stick a love note on my partner's windscreen

✓ Make out in a lift (an idea I copied from the internet)

A bucket list isn't just about ticking boxes.

It's about creating a vision for how you want to live, so that when your time is up, you know you poured yourself into life fully. The act of writing it down brings clarity. Suddenly, your desires and dreams aren't vague thoughts floating in your head, they're concrete intentions waiting to be lived. The benefits are powerful.

A bucket list gives you something to look forward to, no matter how stressful or monotonous life feels. Anticipation itself creates joy. It keeps us motivated through the tough seasons, reminding us that life is more than bills, deadlines, and responsibilities.

It also gives you a sense of progress and fulfilment. Every time you tick something off, whether it's skydiving from 14,000 feet or writing a love note to your partner, you feel a rush of accomplishment. Not the kind you get from a work task or crossing off a to-do list, but the deeper satisfaction that comes from living in alignment with what matters to you.

Most importantly, a bucket list makes you feel alive. It interrupts autopilot living. It's a gentle push to step outside your comfort zone, to laugh harder, to connect deeper, to notice beauty, to savour the simple joys.

It's not about extravagance, it's about presence. And when you look back, your bucket list becomes a collection of stories, not just goals. Stories that make you smile, cry, and laugh. Stories you can pass on to your kids. Stories that remind you: I lived, I loved, I didn't waste this one precious life.

Too many people wait. They wait until the business is stable. Until the kids are older. Until they have more time, more money, more certainty.

But here's the truth: *life doesn't wait.*

I once read about a beautiful young girl named Alice Pyne from the UK who was diagnosed with terminal cancer at 15. Instead of letting fear take over, she made a bucket list: meet her favourite band, swim with sharks, help others sign up as bone marrow donors.

Her list inspired people around the world. And when she passed, her family continued completing her dreams in her honour.

Alice reminded us all: *life is fleeting. But the memories we make are eternal.*

WHY TIMING MATTERS FOR YOUR BUCKET LIST

One impactful book I've read recently was *Die With Zero* by Bill Perkins. His core message? Don't just accumulate money and save experiences for retirement. Instead, spend your time, energy, and money in the right seasons of your life because not all experiences age well.

If you die young, you might regret not truly *living* at all. The idea is to intentionally spend as much of your resources as possible during your lifetime, not hoard them for a "someday" that may never come. He also introduced a concept that really stuck with me: *bucketing your bucket list.*

Some dreams are best experienced in your 20s, 30s, or 40s when your body, energy, and freedom allow for it. Others can wait until later in life. The key is to match your adventures to the stage you're in and make the most of every season.

Example Buckets:

- *In Your 30's & 40's*
  Backpack through Europe
  Try surfing or snowboarding
  Take my parents on a vacation
- *In Your 50's & 60's*
  Learn a new language
  Start mentoring or coaching others
  Travel on a Business Class flight
- *In Your 70's+*
  Host a big birthday on a private island
  Write a memoir
  Travel on a First Class flight

The key takeaway? Don't delay what belongs to this season of life. Some moments, once missed, can't be recaptured. You might still be alive at 70, but maybe your knees won't let you hike Mount Everest anymore. So do it now, while you can.

MAKE IT MEANINGFUL WITH THE 5 LOVE LANGUAGES

When you're creating your bucket list, don't just think about what you want to do. Think about how you can make memories with the people you love. This is where the 5 Love Languages can help guide you. Each person in our life feels most loved in different ways, and knowing this makes it easier to choose experiences that truly matter.

Developed by Dr Gary Chapman, the 5 Love Languages describe the different ways people give and receive love. When you understand them, you can design bucket list moments that go deeper than ticking a box, they create lasting emotional connection. The 5 Love Languages Are:

1. *Words of Affirmation:* Showing love through kind, thoughtful, and encouraging words.
2. *Acts of Service:* Doing something helpful without being asked because love is often shown through actions, not just words.
3. *Receiving Gifts:* Giving a thoughtful present, big or small. It's the intention and meaning that count most.
4. *Quality Time:* Offering your full, undivided attention. Being present is one of the most powerful ways to say "I love you."
5. *Physical Touch:* Expressing affection through hugs, kisses, holding hands, or simply being close.

So when you're adding to your bucket list, especially experiences with others, think about how you can show love in ways that really resonate with them.

Here are some simple, heart-filling ideas to try:

Words of Affirmation

- Write your child a letter they can read when they're older
- Record a video message for your partner or parents for no reason

- Create a gratitude journal for someone and fill it with notes

Acts of Service

- Cook your partner's favourite dish from scratch
- Help a friend launch their dream project
- Clean your parents' house as a surprise gift

Receiving Gifts

- Create a custom photo book of shared memories
- Surprise someone with a "just because" care package
- Gift your partner an experience instead of a material thing

Quality Time

- Plan a tech-free picnic at the park
- Take a road trip with your kids, just you and them
- Schedule monthly date nights or parent-child outings

Physical Touch

- Have cuddle movie nights at home
- Give your partner a kiss every night
- Dance in the living room together.

Start your bucket list today. You don't need to write 100 things right now. But open that Excel sheet or notebook, and begin. Dream freely, without logic or limits. This is your life's highlight reel in the making.

FINAL THOUGHTS

If you died tomorrow, what would you regret not doing? You don't have to wait for the perfect moment. The perfect moment is *right now,* while you're healthy, able, and here.

Because in the end, it's not the money, the titles, or the trophies we'll remember. It's the memories we made. The *people* we loved. The *life* we chose to live fully.

Part of the reason I decided to write this book is because I realised there will never be a "right" time. If I only had twelve months left, sharing my wisdom and experiences with the world is exactly what I'd want to do. So I'm doing it now, before it's too late.

In the next chapter, I'll show you how to make time to actually enjoy your bucket list. Because I know how busy life gets, and how quickly time flies. Let's get intentional about how to optimise our time, so we're not just dreaming about life, but living it.

ACTION STEPS

1. Start your bucket list today, by asking yourself "If I had 12 months to live, what would I like to experience"
2. Bucket your list by age, what should you prioritise now versus later?
3. Ask your loved ones what's on their list and create a shared one.
4. Pick one thing and schedule it this month, big or small, just start.

Section 4. Mastering Time, Energy & Focus

"What gets measured gets managed."
—Peter Drucker

CHAPTER 4.1

Auditing How You Spend Time

If you've ever ended the day feeling exhausted but unsure what you actually accomplished, you're not alone.

This is exactly why auditing your time is one of the most transformational things you can do as an entrepreneur. When you track where your hours really go, you start to see what's aligned and what's just noise.

You begin to let go of what's draining you in business and at home and take back control of your energy, your focus, and ultimately, your life.

THE ILLUSION OF PRODUCTIVITY

I used to assume I was being productive because I was busy all the time. But when I zoomed out and took an honest look, I realised that "busy" and "effective" aren't the same thing.

So much of my time was going to things I could do but shouldn't be doing. An example of a small change that made a huge difference was delegating appointment bookings to my Virtual Assistant (VA).

It sounds simple, but I didn't realise how much time I was spending going back and forth trying to find a time, date, and location for meetings. Then there's the rescheduling, the confirmations, the follow-ups... it all adds up.

Now, my VA handles all of that, and I only show up where I need to be. The time I freed up allowed me to shift back into my zone of genius, i.e. leading, strategising, and creating.

So many entrepreneurs (myself included) fall into the trap of *just doing it themselves* because:

- It's faster
- They've always done it that way
- They don't think anyone else can do it as well
- They don't want to "bother" someone else

But here's the mindset shift: *Just because you can do something, doesn't mean you should.*

I know how to design Canva graphics. I can edit videos. I can book my own appointments. But if I spend my time on all of that, when do I get to do the work that only I can do?

This is where time audits go beyond productivity, they become an *exercise in leadership.*

ASK YOURSELF THESE 3 QUESTIONS

When reviewing your time log, ask:

1. **What are the tasks that only I can do?** (E.g. vision, deep relationships, strategic decisions)
2. **What do I genuinely love doing and do best?** (This is likely your zone of genius where you create the most value with ease)
3. **What tasks bring the highest ROI or impact for the business?** (Not just money but growth, visibility, relationships, long-term traction)

If it doesn't pass at least two out of these three filters, consider:

1. Can I delegate this?
2. Can I stop doing this altogether?
3. Can I automate it?

This is how you protect your time for what matters most.

AUDITING TIME AT HOME TOO

Time audits aren't just for your business. They're just as powerful at home.

For years, I had a cleaner come once a month, thinking that was enough. But even with that support, I still found myself cleaning the other 29 days, tidying up after the kids, doing laundry, and slowly growing frustrated and exhausted. Not to mention the endless arguments with my husband over his expectations around cleanliness.

Eventually, I realised: every hour I spent cleaning was an hour I wasn't truly present with my family. That shift in awareness pushed me to experiment with getting more help.

So I upgraded, first to once a fortnight, then once a week, and eventually five days a week for a couple of hours a day.

Yes, it was an investment, but the return was worth every dollar. I saw it as hiring a part-time employee for under $2,000 a month to free me from domestic duties. The result? More peace. Less stress. And more space for the things that fuel me, like working out, journalling, or simply relaxing. Later, when we moved into a new house with more cupboard space, I also invested in a robot vacuum and mop.

Suddenly, I didn't need as much help, so I reduced the cleaner to three days a week. The point is, you can (and should) adjust your level of support as life changes.

That's when I realised outsourcing is like a muscle you build. You don't have to leap straight to full-time support, start small, get comfortable, and increase over time.

Each step helps you learn to trust others more, to let go without guilt or worry, and to realise that getting the job done 90% to your standard is far better than exhausting yourself chasing perfection.

We often think outsourcing is a luxury. But when you calculate the energy, time, and peace it gives back, you realise it's actually a necessity.

HOW TO AUDIT YOUR TIME

If you've never done a time audit before, here's a simple way to start.

1. Track everything for 3–7 days

Every 30–60 minutes, jot down what you found yourself doing in that block of time. Be honest. Include the "small things" like scrolling social media, tidying up, uploading a video, or answering emails.

2. Sort tasks into categories

Once you've got the data, review your list and group tasks into categories such as:

- *High-value tasks* (things only you can do that move the needle)
- *Low-value tasks* (repetitive admin, errands, chores)
- *Energy-giving* (activities that light you up)
- *Energy-draining* (tasks you dread or that leave you exhausted)

3. Look for patterns

Where are you wasting time? Where are you over-committed? What's missing (time for yourself, family, or strategic thinking)?

4. Decide what to keep, cut, or delegate

Use your audit to decide: What must stay on your plate, what can be eliminated, and what could be handed off.

FINAL THOUGHTS

The goal of a time audit isn't to make you busier, it's to give you clarity. When you see where your hours really go, you can start to plan what to delegate, outsource, or eliminate.

Over time, these small shifts move you from being "busy" to being effective, efficient, and intentional.

And let's be real, we're all busy. The question is: busy doing what? Auditing your time isn't just a productivity hack, it's an identity shift.

It's you stepping fully into your role as:

- A leader.
- A present parent.
- A visionary.
- A rested, creative, joyful human being.

You're not here to survive your to-do list. You're here to build a business and life that feels expansive, intentional, and fulfilling. And it all starts by looking at your hours not with guilt, but with curiosity.

In the next chapter, we'll explore how to overcome the challenges of letting go and step confidently into the art of delegation.

ACTION STEPS

1. **Track Your Time for 3–7 Days**
   Use a spreadsheet, app, or journal. Be honest and detailed.
2. **Audit Your Home Life Too**
   What chores or stressors could you outsource or simplify? Cleaning, groceries, pick-ups?
3. **Let Go of One Task This Week**
   Start with something small. Build the muscle.
4. **Schedule a Quarterly Time Audit**
   Revisit how you spend your time every 3 months to stay aligned with your 5 Pillars.

CHAPTER 4.2

The Art of Delegation

We all start a business wanting more freedom. But the irony? We often end up working more not because we love it, but because we haven't mastered the art of delegation.

The truth is: Success in business and life is a team sport. Whether it's building your business, raising a family, or protecting your mental health, you were never meant to do it all alone.

Delegation is how you reclaim time for your true priorities: faith, family, self-care, and your bigger mission. Letting go isn't giving up control, it's stepping into leadership.

And it's not just something you *try* once. It's something you get better at through consistent auditing and off-loading.

EVEN IF YOU HAVE A TEAM... YOU'RE PROBABLY STILL HOLDING ON

Having a team doesn't mean you're delegating well. In fact, many founders still:

- Review everything before it goes out
- Hold on to their "favourite" tasks because they fear someone else won't do it right
- Feel guilty handing things over

Delegation isn't just a strategy, it's a mindset shift.

You have to believe that your time is best spent on the highest-value work, and that others can rise to the task, if you give them the chance. For a long time, I believed recruiting was *my thing*. After all, I was the original "*Outsourcing Angel*", the one who started it all. I was great at it, and deep down, I didn't think anyone else could match my intuition for choosing the right candidate.

"How could I possibly teach someone to do what I do?" I thought. But here's the truth: Everyone is replaceable, including me. And that's a blessing.

I started documenting my thought process, recording my calls, and letting my team shadow me. Eventually, not only did they become skilled recruiters, they trained others too.

The very thing I thought made me "irreplaceable" became the system that set my business free. When you first hire help, it won't feel easy. Whether you're hiring a local staff member, a virtual assistant, or even a cleaner at home, it won't feel smooth at first.

They won't be as fast. They won't do it as good as you (yet). You'll be tempted to say, "I'll just do it myself." But over time, if you commit to training, communicating, and letting go, they'll get better. They'll become faster.

And eventually, they'll do things you never even thought of. Remember: No one starts off amazing. You didn't either!

THE 30X RULE: TRAIN ONCE, SAVE TIME FOREVER

Rory Vaden, author of *Procrastinate on Purpose*, introduces a powerful concept called the 30X Rule:

> If a task takes you 5 minutes to do, it's worth spending up to 150 minutes (5 x 30) training someone else to do it, even if it feels inefficient at first.

Here's the maths:

- A 5-minute task done daily = 5 × 250 workdays = 1,250 minutes/year (over 20 hours)
- Spend 150 minutes to train someone once = 1250 minutes - 150 minutes = 1,100 minutes saved every year

That's just one task. Now imagine applying that principle to 5 or 10 different areas in your life or business. Delegation is not an expense. It's a compound investment in your freedom.

COMMON HURDLES OF DELEGATION (AND HOW TO OVERCOME THEM)

Even when we know delegation will free us, most of us hit the same roadblocks. Here are the most common hurdles and how to move past them:

1. "No one can do it as well as me."

This mindset keeps you trapped. The truth? They don't need to do it exactly like you, they just need to get it done. 80% right is better than 0% because you never let it go. Over time, with training and feedback, that 80% can turn into 100%.

2. "It's faster if I just do it myself."

Maybe once. But if you keep doing it, you'll be stuck doing it forever. Think of delegation as an investment: you spend time teaching once so you can reclaim that time every week moving forward.

3. "I feel guilty handing this off."

Delegation isn't dumping work, it's giving someone else the chance to grow, contribute, and shine. People often feel more valued when they're trusted with responsibility.

4. "I don't know what to delegate."

Start with the draining, repetitive, or low-value tasks. If it doesn't require your unique genius, it's a candidate for delegation. Use your time audit as your guide.

5. "What if they make mistakes?"

They will. And that's okay. Mistakes are part of the learning curve. Build a feedback loop; check in, improve, and move on. Over time, you'll find they improve and may even bring fresh ideas you hadn't considered.

6. "But what if I can't afford to hire help?"

This is one of the most common resistance points I hear and I get it. When you're early in your business, or cash flow is tight, hiring someone might feel like a luxury you just can't afford. But let me challenge that gently:

You can't afford *not* to delegate because your time is your most valuable asset. If you're stuck doing $20/hour tasks, you're blocking yourself from $200/hour opportunities like sales, strategy, and creating assets that grow your business.

Instead of thinking: "I can't afford help", ask yourself:

1. What's the smallest task I can offload right now?
2. Can I start with just 5 hours a week?
3. Could I barter with someone or use a part-time virtual assistant?
4. What would I gain if I freed up just 1 hour a day?

Delegation is less about skill and more about mindset. The sooner you let go of perfectionism, guilt, and fear, the sooner you'll step into the role you're meant to play: leader, not doer.

HOW TO DELEGATE EFFECTIVELY

So, you're convinced delegation is a must. But how you do it can either make you love it or turn you off it altogether. Delegation isn't about dumping tasks. It's about transferring responsibility with clarity and support, so you can focus on higher-value work. Here's a simple framework:

1. Choose the Right Tasks

Start with the low-value, repetitive, or draining tasks from your time audit. Ask yourself: *Does this really need my brain?* If not, it's a candidate for delegation.

2. Pick the Right Person

Match the task to someone with the right skillset and capacity. If you don't have that person yet, that's your cue for the next hire.

3. Start Small

Don't expect someone to take on everything at once. Break their role into manageable steps.

- For example, a new Sales Rep might first spend time on-boarding and learning about the business. Their first task could simply be calling old leads about a new promotion. Once they succeed, add sales calls. Firstly by shadowing you, then you shadow them, before letting them run solo.
- Similarly, when hiring a cleaner, I don't throw them the whole house at once. I start with the laundry (washing, drying, folding, and putting it away) before adding new responsibilities.

Confusion kills momentum. Overwhelm kills productivity. Starting small builds confidence for both you and them.

4. Give Clear Instructions

Provide context (why it matters), the outcome you expect (what success looks like), and the deadline.

5. Provide Tools & Resources

Make sure they have access to the systems, logins, and templates they'll need. Don't set them up to fail.

6. Set Checkpoints, Not Chains

Agree on how you'll check progress. Daily updates may be necessary at the start, but once trust builds, move to weekly reports. This keeps you in the loop without hovering.

7. Allow for Imperfection

They won't do it exactly like you and that's okay. 80% is enough. With feedback and time, they'll improve, and often bring fresh ideas. Progress beats perfection.

8. Review & Refine

After completion, reflect on what worked and what didn't. Delegation is a muscle, the more you practise it, the stronger (and easier) it gets for both you and them.

CASE STUDY #1: FROM OVERWHELM TO OPTIMISATION -JAMES

James owns a used vehicle sales business and had been running it the same way for nearly three decades: manual paperwork, old-school filing systems, and everything managed by him and his wife.

When he reached out to my team at Outsourcing Angel, his only goal was to hire a virtual assistant to reduce the pressure on himself and his partner.

He started with a 20-hour-per-week VA, mainly to help with admin and online listings. But within a few weeks, the VA didn't just take over repetitive tasks, she introduced new tools like Google Sheets inventory trackers, automated customer follow-ups, and even helped implement AI to qualify leads from Facebook ads.

In just the first two months, James estimated he saved over 30 hours and increased inquiries by 25%. What's more, his wife no longer had to work weekends, and they finally booked their first holiday in years. He said: *"I was hesitant at first, I thought hiring offshore meant lower quality. But now, I'm working less, selling more, and spending real time with my family."*

CASE STUDY #2: DELEGATING AT HOME FOR PEACE AND PRESENCE

A good friend of mine, Emma, used to clean her house every single day on top of running her business, looking after two young kids, and supporting her husband's busy schedule. She often said, *"I feel guilty hiring someone, I should be able to manage it all."*

But deep down, she was exhausted. The constant cleaning made her snappy, disconnected, and frustrated. Her husband noticed it too, and their marriage started to feel more like a functional partnership than a joyful one. Eventually, Emma made the decision to hire a cleaner to come once a fortnight for three hours. The shift was noticeable almost immediately.

With just that small bit of help, she had more time in the mornings, could sit and enjoy a coffee with her husband, and found herself less reactive and more present in the evenings. She's already planning to increase it weekly.

She told me:

> "I thought I was being responsible by doing it all, but letting go gave me back my spark. My husband even commented on how much happier I've been. We laugh more now. We go on walks. Our marriage feels lighter."

Sometimes, the best way to protect what matters most is to get support with the things that don't.

CONSTANTLY REASSESS YOUR CIRCUMSTANCES

Life changes. Business evolves. That's why it's essential to regularly pause and reassess your circumstances.

Ask yourself:

1. What's leaving me exhausted or resentful lately?
2. What used to feel exciting but now feels like a chore?
3. What's stealing time from the things that actually light me up?

Don't wait until burnout creeps in. Let your energy and happiness be your guide. If something consistently feels heavy, draining, or misaligned, it's time to apply the power of the 4Ds.

Label each task with one of the following:

1. **Delete:** If it doesn't move the needle or bring any joy.
2. **Delegate:** If someone else can do it for less than your hourly rate, hand it over.

3. **Decrease:** Do it less often or in shorter, more focused bursts.
4. **Double Down:** This is your zone of genius. Lean into it and do more.

By consistently reassessing and adjusting, you keep your time aligned with your values and your life aligned with what fuels you.

WHAT CAN YOU OUTSOURCE?

By now, you understand that delegation isn't just a business tactic, it's a mindset and a muscle. But here's the next step most people miss: delegation shouldn't stop at work.

True freedom comes when you start thinking about delegation as a whole-life design strategy. It's not just about hiring a virtual assistant to manage your emails; it's about intentionally creating space across every part of your life so you can lead, love, and live fully.

When you delegate well, you're not only freeing time, you're multiplying energy. You're saying, "My time is best spent where it matters most." And that's where 360° Success begins: aligning every pillar of your life so you're not just productive, but fulfilled.

Think about how much lighter you feel when your home runs smoothly, your health routines are organised, your relationships are nurtured, and your travel dreams don't stay stuck on a vision board. Delegation allows all that to happen, not by doing more, but by involving others in your vision.

So instead of asking, "*What can I delegate in my business?*" start asking, *"What can I delegate in my business and life?"*

To help you think holistically, here are 50 examples of what you can delegate across the five pillars of 360° Success, so you can focus on what truly fuels you.

1. Business Freedom

Free your time to work on the business, not in it.

- Inbox and calendar management
- CRM updates, lead tracking, and data entry.
- Preparing reports, presentations, and meeting notes.
- Managing social media posts and engagement.
- Coordinating marketing campaigns and newsletters.
- Booking travel for work events or conferences.
- Invoicing, following up payments, and reconciling receipts.
- Podcast outreach and personal brand building
- Researching competitors, suppliers, or market trends.
- Creating SOPs or documenting processes so your business can run without you.

2. Family Balance

Delegate the little things that make a big difference at home.

- Managing family calendars and school events.
- Organising date nights or family outings.
- Booking appointments; dentist, doctor, car service.
- Paying household bills or tracking budgets.
- Coordinating cleaners, gardeners, or home maintenance.
- Buying gifts for birthdays, holidays, or special occasions.
- Ordering groceries or meal prep kits.
- Managing digital photos or creating memory books and videos
- Planning family holidays and handling logistics.
- Sending thank-you cards or messages on your behalf.

3. Empowered Connections

Delegate ways to nurture relationships and expand your impact.

- Managing your LinkedIn or professional network updates.
- Following up with new contacts after events.

- Researching and organising charitable opportunities.
- Scheduling catch-ups or community involvement.
- Managing your email newsletters or personal brand outreach.
- Tracking birthdays, milestones, and sending appreciation gifts.
- Coordinating collaborations or joint ventures.
- Engaging with online communities that align with your mission.
- Helping you maintain contact with mentors or mentees.
- Organising gratitude initiatives within your team or network.

4. Self-Mastery

Delegate structure around your health, mindset, and growth.

- Booking your gym, yoga, or PT sessions.
- Researching meal plans or healthy recipe ideas.
- Scheduling health check-ups and reminders.
- Managing subscriptions for meditation or learning apps.
- Tracking your progress in fitness or personal goals.

- Ordering supplements or health products.
- Managing your reading list or podcast queue.
- Organising your digital space; files, photos, notes.
- Sending you daily motivational reminders and accountability prompts.
- Coordinating your coaching, therapy, or mastermind sessions.

5. Life Experiences

Delegate to make life more adventurous and joyful.

- Researching travel destinations from your bucket list.
- Booking flights, accommodation, and activities.
- Managing loyalty programs or travel points.
- Creating itineraries for weekends or getaways.
- Finding and booking events, concerts, or retreats.
- Arranging photoshoots or capturing life milestones.
- Creating digital albums, vlogs, or travel journals.
- Finding classes or hobbies; cooking, dancing, surfing.
- Curating surprise experiences for loved ones.
- Managing ticket bookings, restaurants, and local recommendations.

These are just a few examples to spark ideas. How much you can delegate really comes down to your imagination.

You can't outsource someone else to do your workout, because the muscles will end up on them, not you! But almost everything else can be outsourced. The goal is to focus only on what truly adds value to your life and makes you feel happier, lighter, and more fulfilled.

FINAL THOUGHTS

"You can do anything, but not everything." – David Allen

Mastering delegation takes practice. But once you commit to continuous auditing and offloading, your entire life shifts. You free up time for the things that matter. You empower others to rise. And you lead from a place of vision, not just execution.

In Chapter 5.2, I'll show you how you can hire affordable remote talent to help you implement this, so you can build your dream team and start creating true freedom in both business and life.

But first, we'll explore how to use the 80/20 Rule to make smarter decisions and focus only on what creates exponential results.

ACTION STEPS

1. **Delegation Mindset Audit**
   What do you believe about delegating?
   Identify any limiting beliefs
2. **Commit to One Delegation This Week**
   Train someone else using Loom or a checklist this week.
3. **Make Delegation a Habit**
   Every week, ask yourself: "What else can I let go of so I can rise?"

CHAPTER 4.3

Prioritising Using the 80/20 Rule

Focus on less to achieve more. If you've ever felt like you're doing *everything* but still not getting the results you want, this chapter is for you. Because not all tasks are created equal. Not all clients are equal. Not even all hours in the day are equal.

Welcome to the power of the 80/20 Rule, also known as the Pareto Principle. The idea that roughly 80% of results come from 20% of efforts. The key to exponential growth isn't doing more. It's doing more of the right things.

UNDERSTANDING THE 80/20 RULE

Italian economist Vilfredo Pareto discovered that 80% of Italy's land was owned by 20% of the population. Over time, this observation showed up everywhere in business, economics, productivity, and even relationships.

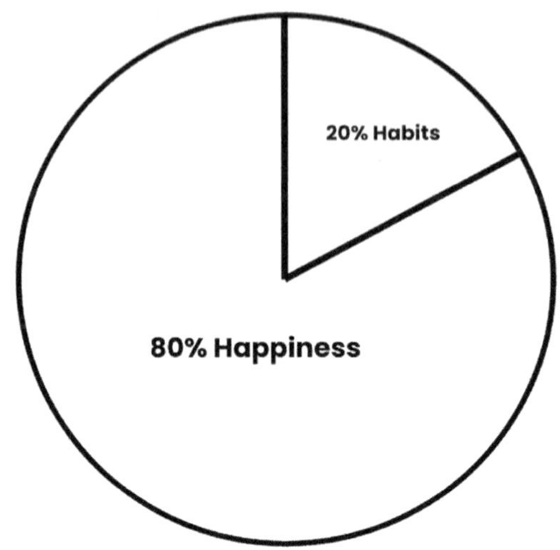

Examples:

- 80% of your revenue likely comes from 20% of your clients
- 80% of your happiness probably comes from 20% of your habits
- 80% of your stress may come from 20% of your tasks

The 80/20 Rule is about finding the vital few and letting go of the trivial many.

SAYING NO TO "GOOD" TO SAY YES TO "GREAT"

There was a season when I said yes to almost every business opportunity, meeting request, and marketing idea. Everything felt important. But I was scattered, overwhelmed, and not getting the traction I wanted. I had to face the truth: I was filling my calendar with "good" things and missing out on the great ones.

When I stepped back and reviewed the numbers, I realised that a small handful of activities like connecting with EO members or hosting my own podcast were delivering the majority of my growth.

So I made a shift: I trained my VA to research and screen opportunities for me. Instead of automatically saying yes to everything, I started saying yes only to what aligned with my goals.

HOW TO APPLY THE 80/20 RULE IN BUSINESS AND LIFE

1. Audit Your Output

Ask yourself:

- What activities generate the most income or impact?
- Which clients or partnerships produce the most results with the least resistance?
- What content platforms give you the best return on time?

Then shift your energy toward the top 20% and reduce or eliminate the bottom 80%.

2. Simplify Your To-Do List

Look at your current to-do list. Now ask:

- If I could only do three things this week to move the needle, what would they be?
- Which tasks are urgent but not impactful?
- What can be automated, delegated, or removed?

You'll realise that most of your "urgencies" are distractions in disguise.

3. Apply It to Your Energy

- Which habits give you 80% of your calm and clarity? (E.g. early wake-ups, journalling, praying, working out)
- Which people or conversations drain 80% of your emotional energy?

It's okay to set boundaries with people, even if they're nice. Your energy is your responsibility.

80/20 AT HOME

This principle isn't just for business. It applies at home too. I realised that:

- 80% of my family stress came from a messy home.
- 80% of my peace came from just a few daily habits; living an alcohol-free life and sticking to my morning routine.

Once I identified that, I rearranged everything to protect those anchors.

I delegated more.
I quit alcohol.
I made sleep a priority and committed to waking up early.

Small changes. Massive peace.

360° SUCCESS LENS

Let's filter your priorities through your 5 Pillars:

Pillars	Ask Yourself
Empowered Connection	1. Who are the 20% of people who help me grow into my best self?
Business Freedom	1. Which 20% of activities buy back 80% of my time and energy? 2. Which 20% of work drives 80% of my income?
Self-Mastery	1. Which 20% of habits fuel 80% of my physical health and daily energy? 2. Which 20% of mindset practices sharpen 80% of my focus, resilience, and mental strength? 3. Which 20% of spiritual practices help me feel most at peace, calm, and guided?
Family Balance	1. What 20% of routines or rituals help me stay most present with my loved ones?
Life Experiences	1. What 20% of experiences bring me the most joy, rest, or fulfilment?

When you know what matters, it's easier to let go of what doesn't.

FINAL THOUGHTS

You don't need a longer to-do list. You need a clearer sense of what actually moves the needle.

The difference between overwhelmed entrepreneurs and successful ones isn't how much they do, it's how well they filter. The 80/20 Rule is the filter that sets you free.

In the next chapter, we'll look at how to time-block for energy, not just productivity so you can protect your most focused hours for your most important work.

ACTION STEPS

1. **Spot the 20% that matters most**
   Review your calendar, habits, and commitments through the lens of the 80/20 rule. Which few activities create the biggest results, joy, or progress? Which are just noise?
2. **Eliminate or Delegate the Trivial Many**
   Choose at least 3 low-impact or time-wasting tasks you can cut or hand off this week. Freeing space is what allows the 20% to flourish.
3. **Define Your Daily "Top 3"**
   Each morning, identify the 3 highest-leverage tasks that most likely move the needle. That becomes your new Must-Do List. Everything else is optional.

CHAPTER 4.4

Time-Blocking for Energy, Not Just Tasks

You've probably heard this before: *"If it's not in your calendar, it won't happen."* But here's the deeper truth: If it's in your calendar at the wrong time, it might never happen (at least not well).

Traditional time-blocking tells us to assign tasks to time slots. But high performers don't just manage their time. They manage their energy. And when you do that? You stop hustling your way through the day and start flowing with clarity, calm, and impact.

THE PRODUCTIVITY TRAP: BUSY ≠ EFFECTIVE

You can have a beautifully colour-coded calendar and still feel burnt out. Why? Because not all hours are created equal. Some hours you're sharp and on fire. Other hours? You're foggy, distracted, or just plain done.

The mistake isn't that we're not planning. It's that we're planning against our energy rhythms. Think of it like this:

Would you schedule a deep strategy session during your post-lunch slump? Or try to have a heart-to-heart with your child right after a stressful day? Probably not. But that's exactly what most calendars force us into.

MY ENERGY SHIFT

For years, I followed the common advice: *"work out first thing in the morning."* So the moment I woke up, I'd rush to the gym. But I realised something important; my mind is razor sharp in the early hours. That's my golden window. I can solve complex problems or write brilliant content in a fraction of the time it takes later in the day. And every time I used that peak energy on a workout, my brain would buzz with ideas I couldn't capture.

On the flip side, if I pushed the gym to later, I'd procrastinate or cancel altogether. So I switched it up. Now I start at 4am with deep, creative work, the kind that truly moves my business forward. Then, around 6am, I transition into my workout with a clear head and a sense of accomplishment. That flow fuels both my mind and my body, without either competing for my best energy.

Hard work first. Then hard workouts. Before the world needs me.

That simple shift changed everything about how I show up and made me fall in love with mornings.

TRACK YOUR ENERGY BEFORE YOU BLOCK YOUR TIME

Before you plan your week, spend 3–5 days mapping your natural rhythms.

Use this scale every few hours:

- High Energy (clear, focused, creative)
- Medium Energy (functional, admin-ready)
- Low Energy (tired, unfocused, easy tasks)

Then match your work to your energy:

Task Type	Best Energy Match	Examples
Strategy, content, decisions	High	Visioning, writing, planning
Admin, email, meetings	Medium	Updates, calls, reporting
Maintenance, errands, wrap-up	Low	Filing, inbox zero, tidying up systems

CREATE THEMED DAYS TO REDUCE DECISION FATIGUE

Another great tool I use is themed days, giving each weekday a focus. This minimises context-switching and creates more flow by batching similar types of energy together.

I personally group my work into what I call the 4 Cs:

- **Content** – Days dedicated to podcasts, recording, and shooting content.
- **Connection** – Days for networking, external meetings, and relationship-building.
- **Culture** – Days focused on internal team meetings and working closely with my team.
- **Clarity** – I use my early mornings for thinking about vision, strategic planning, and big problem-solving.

Themed days help me stay in a creative or strategic flow, rather than constantly shifting gears. Here are some ideas you can adapt to your own rhythm:

Day	Theme	Focus
Monday	Leadership & Planning	Team syncs, priority setting
Tuesday	Content & Creation	Writing, Recording, Ideas
Wednesday	Coaching Days	Coaching, Training
Thursday	Business Development	Sales calls, partnerships, networking

Friday	CEO Time	Visioning, Reviewing, Reflection
Saturday/ Sunday	Rest, Faith & Family	Bonding, Connecting, Experiences

ADD BUFFER, RECOVERY, AND INTEGRATION TIME

According to Cal Newport, author of Deep Work, even the most focused individuals only have 4–6 hours of real cognitive productivity per day. That's why space between blocks is just as important as the tasks themselves. Block these in:

- 10–15 mins between meetings
- A reset break after deep work
- A short walk between calls
- An end-of-day ritual to signal "off time"

Don't fill every minute. Design your days to breathe.

TIME-BLOCK FOR YOUR PILLARS, TOO

Most people fill their calendars only with "work stuff": meetings, deadlines, and endless to-do lists. But to truly achieve 360° Success, your calendar should reflect your 5 Pillars, not just your career goals.

Your schedule shouldn't only show what you have to do. It should show what matters most to you.

If you don't intentionally create space for all areas of life, work will always expand to fill every gap and everything else gets squeezed into the margins.

Pillar	Energy-Based Time Ideas
Empowered Connection	Schedule catch-up calls, networking meetings, or lunch dates during late mornings or early afternoons when your social energy is naturally higher.
Business Freedom	Block high-energy times (typically mid-morning) for strategy work, revenue-generating activities, or leadership meetings not low-value admin tasks.
Self-Mastery	Protect your early mornings for quiet, focused practices like prayer, journalling, reflection, reading, or workouts when your mind is freshest.
Family Balance	Reserve tech-free evenings for family dinners, scheduled family check-ins, and one-on-one time with kids when everyone naturally winds down.
Life Experiences	Plan monthly "Joy Days," weekend adventures, or holidays during weekends or planned downtime to fully recharge and reconnect without pressure.

SMART TIME BATCHING: ONE ACTION, MULTIPLE WINS

Once you've blocked time for each pillar, here's a powerful upgrade: combine them. You don't always need more time, just smarter time. When you stack activities that nourish multiple pillars, you create a ripple effect of alignment with less effort.

Here are some ways I batch for fulfilment:

- **Friendship + Fitness:** I do online workouts with friends once every week for the purpose connecting with my friends while getting fit at the same time.
- **Learning + Movement:** I listen to audio books or podcasts while walking outdoors. It keeps my mind sharp and my body active, with minimal extra time required.
- **Business + Life Experience + Connection:** I travel with my team to new destinations. While we're ticking off business goals, we're also creating memories, exploring new places, and deepening relationships all at once.

Think of it as life layering. Next time you're planning your week, ask: *"What's one activity that could hit two or more pillars at once?"*

FINAL THOUGHTS

Your calendar is a mirror. If it reflects stress and disconnection, it's time to redesign it. If it reflects clarity, peace, and impact then you're living in alignment.

Stop asking how to get more done. Start asking: "When do I feel most alive to do my best work?" Then build a week that supports that version of you.

In the next chapter, we'll explore how to design a business that can thrive without you at the centre.

ACTION STEPS

1. **Track Your Energy for 3–5 Days**
   Every 2–3 hours, log whether your energy is high, medium, low
2. **Design a Week Based on Energy Zones**
   Place high-focus tasks in high-energy slots. Move admin and low-impact tasks to low-energy times.
3. **Theme Your Days**
   Create a simple theme per weekday to reduce context switching and decision fatigue.

Section 5: Building a Business That Runs Without You

"If you don't build systems, you are the system."
— Dave Jenyns

CHAPTER 5.1

Systemising Your Business for Scale

If you ever want true freedom from your business whether it's for travel, rest, family time, or to pursue your next big vision, you need one thing above all: *systems.*

Systems are what separate entrepreneurs who are constantly putting out fires from those who grow with ease and clarity. They're how you stop being the only one who knows how things work and start building a machine that runs without your daily input.

> *"You don't rise to the level of your goals. You fall to the level of your systems."* -James Clear

According to McKinsey & Company, companies that embrace systemisation and process automation see up to a 30% reduction in operational costs and a significant increase in team productivity. Systemising is not just for corporate giants, it's a competitive advantage that small businesses can't afford to ignore.

Let's break this down into practical, scalable moves.

WHAT DOES IT MEAN TO SYSTEMISE?

Systemising doesn't mean turning your business into a soulless factory. It means:

- Creating repeatable processes for repeatable tasks
- Documenting how things are done so others can follow
- Using tools to automate wherever possible
- Reducing decision fatigue by having clear workflows

In short: it's giving your business a memory.

Harvard Business Review reports that employees spend nearly 20% of their time looking for internal information or tracking down colleagues to help with tasks. That's one full day a week lost, simply due to a lack of structure. When you systemise, you reclaim that lost time.

CHAOS IS EXPENSIVE

Early in my business, everything lived in my head. I'd repeat myself daily, show every new staff member how to do things manually, and scramble to fix mistakes because there were no standard ways of working.

I thought I was saving time by just doing things myself or showing people on the fly. But really, I was creating dependency and bottlenecks. The game changed when I committed to building systems. I started documenting processes, recording Loom video tutorials, and saving templates in shared folders.

What once felt overwhelming started to feel repeatable and scalable. I saw faster onboarding, fewer errors, and most importantly, I finally had the breathing room to work on growing the business instead of just running it.

WHAT TO SYSTEMISE FIRST

Start with what's *frequent and frustrating*. Ask yourself:

- What tasks are repeated weekly or monthly?
- Where do mistakes or delays often happen?
- What am I constantly asked about or needed for?

Examples might include:

- Client onboarding
- Invoicing and payment tracking
- Responding to common customer queries

Remember: If you do something more than twice, it deserves a process. Here's how to get started:

- Choose one task you do regularly that someone else could eventually take over.
- Record yourself doing it using Loom, or take screenshots and outline the steps as you go. You can try AI tools like scribehow.com or bit.ai that can speed up the process.
- Get your team involved. You don't have to create every system yourself. Your role is to identify what needs documenting and delegate the creation of SOPs when possible.
- Store it in one central place like Google Drive, Notion, or specific SOP tool.

Start small. One Standard Operating Process (SOP) at a time. Over time, you'll build a library that gives you true freedom.

As Michael Gerber explains in *The E-Myth Revisited, "The system runs the business, and the people run the system."* Without documented processes, your business relies on memory and guesswork neither of which scale.

FINAL THOUGHTS

You can't scale chaos. And you don't have to.

Systemisation is the bridge between hustle and freedom. The more you document and simplify, the more you empower your team and your future self to thrive.

> *"The more your business depends on you, the less it's worth. The more it depends on systems, the more it's worth."* -John Warrillow, author of *Built to Sell*

In the next chapter, we'll explore how to build a team that can run these systems so you can stop being the glue and start being the guide.

ACTION STEPS

1. Pick one recurring task you still handle.
2. Record yourself doing it this week.
3. Turn it into a step-by-step guide.
4. Save it somewhere your team can access.
5. Rinse and repeat.

CHAPTER 5.2

Leveraging Remote Team Support

If you have systemised your processes, the next step is simple: do not run those systems yourself.

Too many entrepreneurs create great SOPs but still act as the bottleneck. Real freedom comes when you empower others, especially your remote team, to own and operate the systems you have built.

When I talk about team, I do not just mean anyone working from home. I mean offshore team members, skilled professionals in developing countries such as the Philippines.

They can take on almost any role or task that can be done online, running your systems for you while you focus on growing the business instead of being trapped in it.

The Philippines in particular has one of the most talented and values driven talent pools in the world. Filipinos are highly educated, fluent in English, culturally aligned with Western businesses, and known for their loyalty and work ethic. And because the cost of living is lower, you can hire exceptional people for 50 to 70 percent less than a local equivalent while still paying them above average wages in their own country.

It is a true win–win: business owners gain access to skilled, reliable support, while offshore staff get stable, well paid roles with opportunities that may not exist locally. This shift is not just about saving money, it is about scalability. Offshore talent allows you to reduce overheads, hire flexibly across time zones, scale up or down depending on projects, and support your local team so they do not burn out. With the right structure and communication, they are just as productive, if not more, than in-house employees. I have experienced this first hand.

I started building my business from home while raising kids, long before remote work was mainstream, and I have never looked back. Some of my team members have been with me for over a decade.

Take Wendy, for example, she began as a copywriter but has grown into the role of General Manager, now overseeing the business and managing all finances. Her journey proves that when you invest in the right remote team, they do not just support you, they grow with you. That is the heart of what we do at my company Outsourcing Angel.

We recruit skilled, reliable, and values-aligned remote talent ranging from executive assistants and marketing support to operations leads, so business owners can grow without the growing pains.

Tim Ferriss popularised the idea of virtual assistants in his book, The *4 Hour Workweek,* showing the world that you do not have to do everything yourself to succeed. I took that concept further, building a company that specialises in helping entrepreneurs access offshore talent in a structured, sustainable way. Today, I run a business with over 100 remote staff supporting clients around the world. And I still get to be present with my family.

Even if you already have local employees, adding remote teams is one of the smartest moves you can make. They can take care of admin, research, customer service, content, and follow up work, freeing your local team to focus on their highest value tasks.

A hybrid model of local and offshore talent gives you flexibility, productivity across time zones, and the ability to scale without massive overheads.

I have seen countless businesses thrive by pairing their in-house leaders with dedicated offshore talent. It creates breathing room, protects culture, and allows your best people to work at their best level.

THE ROLES YOU SHOULD DELEGATE FIRST

Too often, business owners assume they can only offload low-level admin. That is a huge mistake.

The global talent pool is full of highly skilled professionals who can step into roles with the expertise and experience you need right now.

Here are some of the first roles to consider if you are feeling stretched:

- **Executive Assistant:** Calendar management, inbox organisation, travel bookings, CRM Management.
- **Marketing Assistant:** Content scheduling, social media posting, repurposing material across platforms.
- **Client Support:** Handling customer queries, sending on-boarding emails, managing FAQs.
- **Operations Support:** Overseeing projects, coordinating weekly task flows, preparing reports.

The goal is to remove the $10-$40 an hour tasks from your plate so you can focus on the $1000 an hour decisions.

By hiring people who already have the skillset to deliver, you can plug them into your systems quickly, reduce your stress, and free yourself to operate as the leader of your business.

BUILDING A CULTURE REMOTELY

You might be thinking, hiring remote teams sounds great, but how do I actually make it work? How do I ensure they fit into my company culture or work effectively if I do not see them in person?

Having worked with remote teams for over a decade, I can tell you this: great culture can be built and sustained whether your team is in the same office or spread across the world.

Culture is not about free lunches or beanbags in the office. It is about how people feel when they show up to work. Do they feel trusted, valued, and empowered? That is what matters most, especially in a remote environment where those feelings become the glue that holds everything together.

One framework I love comes from Tony Robbins: the 6 Human Needs: Certainty, Variety, Significance, Connection, Growth, and Contribution.

These needs apply just as much to your team as they do in life. When you consciously build systems, communication, and recognition that meet these needs, your remote team will not just perform tasks, they will thrive and stay loyal.

When building culture, keep these needs in mind:

1. *Certainty:* How can your team feel secure about their job and career? Clear systems, role expectations, regular feedback, consistent communication rhythms and getting paid on time help build a sense of stability.

2. *Variety:* As much as people crave certainty, they also need variety to stay engaged. Opportunities for learning, creativity, and new challenges keep energy and excitement high.
3. *Significance:* People need to feel that what they do matters. Recognise contributions often and celebrate wins publicly and personally.
4. *Connection:* Strong teams are built on real relationships. Prioritise building rapport, celebrating birthdays, organise team building activities, and doing regular personal check-ins, not just work updates.
5. *Growth:* Offer personal development opportunities, ongoing training, mentorship, and career pathways so your team feels they're moving forward, not stuck.
6. *Contribution:* Everyone wants to feel like they're part of something bigger. Remind your team of the purpose and impact behind the work they do, how they're contributing to a vision larger than themselves. Align your business with a charity or give back initiatives (check out propurpose.org).

Do not let culture become a buzzword, make sure it is lived day to day. Bad culture develops through unclear roles, lack of follow through on feedback, celebrating hustle while neglecting well-being, and no space for vulnerability or personal connection. In a remote environment, these gaps are magnified. People do not leave jobs, they leave unclear expectations, lack of recognition, and no growth path.

Whether you are hiring a contractor, offshore team, or someone part-time, treat them like you would your in house team. Take the long term view. Invest in training. Give them room to make mistakes and learn. Be loyal to them, and they will be loyal to you.

One of the biggest mistakes business owners make is seeing outsourced talent as temporary or disposable. But when you treat them as trusted members of your team with clear expectations, consistent support, and room to grow, they will treat your business like it is their own.

I have had team members stay with me for over a decade because they feel valued, supported, and included.

When I am travelling or stepping away from the business, I know they have it covered, not just because it is their job, but because they care.

REMOTE TOOLS THAT HELP TEAMS THRIVE

Culture and people are the heart of a remote team, but without the right tools even the best culture will struggle to survive.

Communication can break down, projects can get lost in emails, and collaboration becomes messy fast. What allows a remote team to truly thrive is having the right systems and tools in place to keep everyone connected, aligned, and productive.

Here are the essentials I recommend:

1. Communication

- *Slack, Google Chats or Microsoft Teams:* For instant messaging and quick check-ins that replace office chatter.
- *Zoom or Google Meet:* For face-to-face video calls to maintain connection and clarity.
- *Loom:* For creating video instructions or SOPs straight from your desktop

2. Project and Task Management

- *Asana, Trello, or Notion:* To manage tasks, assign responsibilities, and track progress. These tools keep everyone on the same page and eliminate the "who's doing what" confusion.

3. File Sharing and Collaboration

- *Google Workspace or Notion:* For documents, spreadsheets, and presentations that can be edited in real time.
- *Google Drive or Dropbox:* For storing larger files securely.

4. Time and Productivity

- *Time Doctor or Hubstaff:* For tracking hours and measuring productivity.
- *Toggl:* A simple time-tracking tool for freelancers or project-based work.

5. Culture and Connection

- *Donut (Slack add-on):* Pairs team members randomly for virtual coffee chats to build relationships.
- *Kudos boards or Bonusly:* For peer-to-peer recognition and celebrating wins.

6. Automation

- *Zapier or Make:* To connect apps and automate repetitive processes so your team spends less time on busywork.

Remember, tools are only as good as the systems behind them. I will share even more tools in the next chapter to show you how to use technology for a smarter, more efficient working environment.

FINAL THOUGHTS

A remote team isn't just an "extra set of hands", they're your force multiplier.

When empowered, they become the engine that runs your business while you focus on where you're most needed. In the next chapter, we'll explore how to scale your efficiency even further by using technology and AI to do the heavy lifting behind the scenes.

ACTION STEPS

1. Identify 3 tasks you currently do that could be handled remotely.
2. Create a job description for a VA or remote hire.
3. Record a Loom walk through for a process you'll delegate.
4. Book in a call with my Outsourcing Angel team if you want help hiring your remote team.

CHAPTER 5.3

Streamlining Operations with Technology

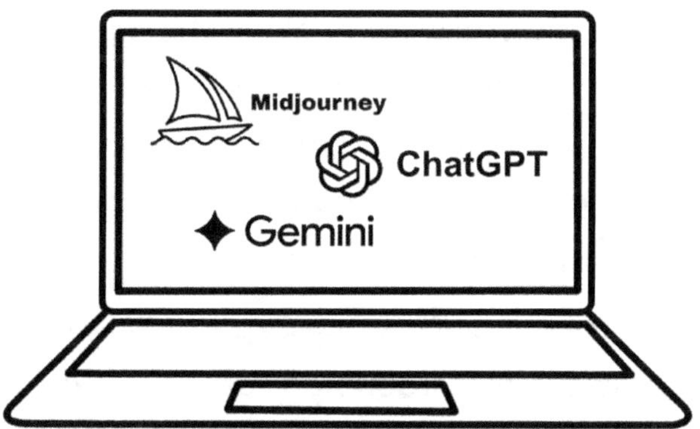

If you want to operate smarter, not harder, you need to embrace the tools that free up your time and reduce your workload. Software, AI, and automation are no longer nice-to-haves. They are essential for creating a scalable, efficient, and modern business.

Whether it is cutting admin time, improving team performance, or enhancing customer experience, AI and automation allow you to work less while achieving more.

Too many business owners are still stuck doing things manually, simply because they do not realise there is a faster way. When you layer the right technology on top of great systems and a strong team, that is when real leverage happens.

I have personally saved dozens of hours each week using just a handful of tools. One of my favourites is ChatGPT. It is like having a strategist, writer, and problem solver in your pocket, available 24/7.

In business and life, ChatGPT has become my all-in-one partner for speed, clarity, and research. I use it to break down Bible verses for deeper understanding and to help me research and write this very book. On the personal side, I treat ChatGPT like my own personal trainer. I tell it my fitness goals and it designs workouts and meal plans around them. I can even upload photos of my meals and it estimates what I ate and how many calories I consumed.

It keeps a record of my actual progress versus my goals, reminds me what to focus on tomorrow, and keeps me accountable day by day. It truly is like having a PT in my pocket, available anytime. I often dictate thoughts while walking or driving and get instant responses in text or voice. It keeps me moving forward in both business and life, even when I am on the go.

Let me show you exactly how I use AI in practical ways, and then I will share a full list of over 100 AI tools you can use to streamline every part of your business operations.

PROMPTS THAT UNLOCK AI'S FULL POWER

Here are some example prompts you can use with ChatGPT for your business and life to get the most out of the tool.

Marketing

"Write a follow-up email to a lead who ghosted me."

"Give me 10 creative angles for a social media campaign about delegation."

Leadership

"Draft a message to boost team morale during a tough month."

"Write a job ad for a proactive remote executive assistant."

Productivity

"Suggest a weekly schedule that gives me 3 days of deep work."

"What are 10 things I should delegate as a founder?"

Family

"Give me conversation starters for family dinners to help my kids open up about their day."

"Create a monthly family activity calendar with one adventure, one learning activity, and one stay-at-home bonding activity each week."

Health

"Design a progressive 4-week workout plan for fat loss and muscle toning, 4 days a week."

These are just a few examples, the possibilities are limitless. The only real boundary is your imagination, because you can ask ChatGPT anything and it will rise to meet you.

USING AUTOMATION TO FREE UP TIME

Beyond ChatGPT, you can pair your team and systems with automation. This will unlock serious time savings and eliminate repetitive work that slows you down.

Tools like Zapier and Make allow you to connect your apps together so they can "talk" to each other automatically without needing any coding experience.

You can set up simple or advanced triggers, such as:

- When a new lead comes through Facebook Ads, automatically add their details to your CRM.
- When someone books a call via calendar app Calendly, send a confirmation email and log the call in Google Sheets.
- Sync leads from your website to your CRM and email platform at once.
- Auto-generate weekly client reports without lifting a finger.
- Trigger complex workflows based on conditions (e.g., only update a task if a deal is over $5,000).

EXAMPLES OF AUTOMATION IN ACTION:

1. **Sales:** Lead fills out a form -> CRM updated -> Welcome email sent -> Slack notification to the sales rep.
2. **Operations:** Proposal signed -> Project created in the system -> Tasks automatically assigned -> Invoice generated.
3. **Content:** Upload a YouTube video -> Summary extracted -> Clips auto-posted to social media -> Content calendar updated.

With a few well-placed automations, you can cut hours of admin each week and keep your business running smoothly in the background while you and your team focus on higher value work.

100+ AI TOOLS TO SUPERCHARGE YOUR BUSINESS

Let's face it, running a business today without leveraging AI is like trying to build a house with a spoon. Whether you're a solopreneur or leading a large team, there are AI tools available right now that can save you time, reduce costs, and improve quality across every department.

Below is a curated list of powerful tools categorised by function, from content and design to automation and analytics. You don't need to use them all. Just start with what solves your biggest bottleneck right now.

1. Research & Strategy Tools

Use these to explore new markets, validate ideas, and gather insights faster than ever.

- *YouChat* – AI powered search engine with sources
- *Abacus* – Financial modelling made simple
- *Perplexity* – Research assistant with real time citations
- *Copilot (GitHub)* – Coding assistant for software projects
- *Gemini* – Google's AI search and research assistant

2. Image Creation & Editing

Perfect for quick visuals, ad creatives, and mockups without a graphic design team.

- *Fotor* – Easy photo editing and graphic design
- *Stability AI* – Open source image generation
- *Midjourney* – Stunning artistic images via Discord
- *Microsoft Designer* – Drag and drop image editing with AI suggestions
- *Typeset* – Turn text into graphics in seconds

3. Copywriting & Content Generation

These tools help you write faster, clearer, and more persuasively.

- *Rytr* – Fast content generator for blogs and ads
- *Copy AI* – Great for sales pages and email copy
- *Writesonic* – Versatile content for websites and social media

4. Writing & Editing Helpers

For polishing content, improving grammar, and writing better, faster.

- *Jasper* – AI writing assistant for marketing teams
- *HIX AI* – All in one AI writer with templates
- *Jenny AI* – Focused on long form content
- *Textblaze* – Text expansion and automation snippets
- *Quillbot* – Rewording and grammar checking made simple

5. Website Builders

Launch landing pages or full sites with ease, no developer needed.

- *Replit* – Turn ideas into an app
- *10Web* – AI powered WordPress builder
- *Durable* – Build a business website in under a minute

- *Framer* – Modern no code website builder
- *Style AI* – AI driven site design custom to your brand
- *Lovable AI* - AI build your site in minutes

6. Video Creation & Editing

Turn raw footage into polished content with minimal effort.

- *Klap* – Auto create short video clips for social
- *Opus.pro* – Video repurposing at scale
- *Glasp* – Auto summarise YouTube videos
- *InVideo* – Templates for pro looking videos
- *HeyGen* – Create talking head videos from text
- *Runway* – AI powered video editing and special effects
- *ImgCreator AI* – Generate illustrations and animations
- *Morphstudio.xyz* – AI avatars and characters
- *Loom* – Screen record videos with AI summaries

7. Meeting Productivity Tools

Capture notes, generate summaries, and never miss a detail again.

- *Tldv* – Automatically records and summarises meetings
- *Otter* – Real time transcription and searchable notes

- *Fathom* – AI assistant that records, transcribes, and extracts key points

8. SEO & Search Optimisation

Grow organic traffic and improve your search visibility.

- *VidIQ* – Optimise YouTube videos
- *Seona AI* – Real time on page SEO analysis
- *BlogSEO* – Find keywords and optimise content
- *Keywords AI* – Keyword research powered by AI

9. Chatbots & Customer Support

Provide instant, smart responses and automate support.

- *Droxy* – Custom GPT chatbots for your site
- *Chatbase* – Train a chatbot on your data
- *Mutual Info* – AI powered customer service
- *Chatsimple* – Instant customer interaction bot

10. Presentation Design

Create beautiful, engaging presentations in minutes.

- *Decktopus* – Build and share presentations fast
- *Slides AI* – Convert text into slides automatically
- *Gamma AI* – Stunning storytelling slides
- *Designs AI* – All in one creative tool
- *Beautiful AI* – Smart templates and design suggestions

11. Automation Platforms

Let your tools talk to each other and run tasks on autopilot.

- *Make* – Advanced visual automation builder
- *Zapier* – Popular no code integration tool
- *Xembly* – Automates meeting scheduling and task follow up
- *Bardeen* – Personal productivity automation
- *n8n* – Flexible AI workflow automation
- *Glean* - Build AI Agents that reflect, plan, and act autonomously.

12. Prompt Libraries

Get better results from AI with curated, powerful prompts.

- *FlowGPT* – Prompt sharing community
- *Alicent AI* – AI prompt explorer
- *PromptBox* – Save and organise your best prompts
- *Promptbase* – Buy and sell high performing prompts
- *Snack Prompt* – Daily prompt inspiration

13. UI/UX Design

Design beautiful, intuitive user interfaces faster.

- *Figma* – Collaborative interface design
- *Uizard* – Turn sketches into mockups
- *UiMagic* – Generate interfaces with prompts

14. Graphic Design Tools

For social media, posters, logos, and everything visual.

- *Canva Magic Studio* – Drag and drop graphic design with AI features
- *Flair AI* – AI styled product photography
- *Designify* – Remove backgrounds and enhance photos
- *Clipdrop* – Background remover and image enhancer
- *Autodraw* – Sketch to graphic conversion
- *Magician Design* – AI tools for Figma

15. Logo Creation

Launch your brand with a professional look in minutes.

- *Looka* – Brand kits and logos
- *Designs AI* – Quick and modern logo options
- *Brandmark* – AI generated logo suggestions
- *Stockimg AI* – Generate mockups and logo previews

16. Voice & Audio Tools

Create voiceovers, podcasts, and more with AI.

- *Lovo AI* – Realistic AI voiceovers
- *Eleven Labs* – Clone and generate human like voices

- *Songburst AI* – Music and jingles made with AI
- *Adobe Podcast* – Enhance poor quality audio
- *Suno* – Make any songs you can imagine

17. Marketing & Ad Tools

Create and test marketing campaigns with ease.

- *Pencil* – Ad creative that learns and improves
- *Ai Ads* – Campaigns built with AI insight
- *AdCopy* – AI powered headline and CTA generator
- *Simplified* – Design, copy, and marketing suite
- *AdCreative* – AI ad visual and copy in one

18. Startup Tools

Get your ideas off the ground and pitch ready.

- *Tome* – Beautiful pitch decks
- *Ideas AI* – Business ideas on demand
- Namelix – AI business name generator
- Pitchgrade – AI grading for startup pitches
- Validator AI – Idea validation through AI

19. Productivity Boosters

Improve your workflow, reduce distraction, and get more done.

- *Merlin* – AI overlay for any browser
- *Tinywow* – One click file conversions

- *Notion AI* – Turn Notion into your second brain
- *Adobe Sensei* – AI engine for Adobe productivity
- *Personal AI* – Your memory assistant
- *Fyxer* – Email management with AI
- *Reclaim* – Smart calendar and time management tool

20. Social Media Management

Schedule posts, repurpose content, and grow faster.

- *Taplio* – LinkedIn content and analytics
- *Typefully* – Twitter post planner
- *Hypefury* – Content scheduling for engagement
- *TweetHunter* – AI powered tweets that convert
- Blaze AI - AI that clones your tone of voice and creates content

FINAL THOUGHTS

I'm not sharing this huge list of tools to overwhelm you, I'm showing you what's possible. There truly is a tool for everything. And the right ones will save you countless hours, reduce manual work, and empower both you and your team to operate smarter, not harder.

Don't settle for "business as usual." Challenge yourself to ask, *"How can I do this differently?"* The truth is, modern technology isn't just for big companies or techies. It's for anyone who's ready to stop being the bottleneck and start building a business that runs with more freedom and flow.

When you learn to work with technology rather than against it, you unlock a new level of speed, clarity, and control.

It's not about cramming more into your day, it's about making space for what matters most by letting systems and tools handle the rest. Your time is too valuable to waste on things that could be automated. Embrace the tools. Embrace the change. And watch your business (and life) transform.

ACTION STEPS

Here are 5 practical ways to start implementing what you've learned:

1. **Audit Your Repetitive Tasks**
   List out the top 10 recurring tasks you or your team do manually. Which of these could be automated?
2. **Sign Up for ChatGPT**
   Use it this week to write a piece of content, brainstorm an idea, or get clarity on a problem. Test different prompts.
3. **Explore 3 New AI Tools**
   From the directory in this chapter, pick 3 tools and spend 30 minutes each exploring how they work. Try one in your workflow.
4. **Set Up One Automation Using Make or Zapier**
   Choose a process you can automate, such as lead capture, email follow-ups, or task creation. Build one automation this week.
5. **Assign Tech Roles in Your Team**
   Who on your team can become your "AI Champion"? Empower someone to explore.

CHAPTER 5.4

Becoming the CEO, Not the Doer

In previous chapters, we talked about building a business that runs without you by focusing on People, Process, and Technology. But there's one more shift that ties it all together: *Your identity as the business owner.* At some point, every entrepreneur has to make a conscious decision to stop being the doer and start fully becoming the CEO.

This isn't just about job titles. It's about mindset, boundaries, and how you show up in your business. If you don't make the shift from doer to CEO, your business will always revolve around you and eventually, that becomes a trap.

You'll find yourself:

- Working longer hours, constantly putting out fires instead of building for the future
- Burnt out, juggling too many hats and never having real time off

- Stuck in the weeds, doing tasks someone else could do better or faster
- Blocking growth, because nothing can scale if it depends on you
- Losing passion, as the weight of daily operations drowns out your creativity and joy

Here's the hard truth: your business cannot outgrow your leadership.

If you don't rise up into your true role as the visionary and architect, you'll build yourself a job, not a business.

And the worst part? You'll become the reason it can't grow. The shift isn't just about delegation only, it's about identity. You have to see yourself as a leader who builds systems, develops people, and protects space to think. You can either keep doing it all... Or you can build something that outlives and outperforms you.

THE REAL ROLE OF A CEO

Gino Wickman, author of Traction and creator of the Entrepreneurial Operating System (EOS), defines the visionary CEO as the person who sets the big picture direction, fosters culture, and makes high-level decisions while the integrator (your second-in-command) ensures the business runs smoothly.

A true CEO focuses on:

- *Vision:* Setting the direction for where the business is going
- *Strategy:* Deciding what to prioritise and what to say no to
- *People:* Hiring leaders, building culture, and managing accountability
- *Cash:* Overseeing financial health and decision-making
- *Systems:* Creating a business that can operate without daily intervention

If you're still buried in task lists, operations, and customer issues then you're likely stuck in the operator zone, not yet owning your CEO role.

FROM OPERATOR TO ORCHESTRATOR

This was one of the biggest shifts I had to make in my own business journey. For years, I wore all the hats: sales, marketing, client support, invoicing, even HR. I thought that was what made me a "hands-on" founder.

But deep down, I was exhausted and frustrated. No matter how much I grew the company, I didn't feel free.

It wasn't until I realised *freedom doesn't come from growth, it comes from letting go.*

That meant hiring my COO (Integrator) to help me execute the vision and keep the day-to-day operations aligned and moving. It was one of the most empowering decisions I made. We didn't stop there, I also began empowering my leadership team, giving them the ownership and tools to make decisions without needing my constant input. I moved from being a bottleneck to being a sounding board and strategic coach.

Today, I focus on things only I can do:

- Leading culture
- Setting the vision
- Nurturing key partnerships
- Content creation and brand presence
- Coaching and developing my leadership team

Everything else? I've either delegated, automated, or eliminated.

The CEO Scorecard

Here's how to assess if you're truly functioning as a CEO:

Area	Doer Mode	CEO Mode
Time	Spent in operations and reactive tasks	Spent in strategy, vision, leadership, and deep thinking
Focus	Task completion, urgent issues	High-leverage decisions, long-term growth
Team	Micromanaging or bottlenecking	Empowering leaders, clear KPIs and outcomes
Meetings	Back-to-back status updates	Strategic discussions and performance check-ins
Calendar	Fully booked, no white space	Intentional, with CEO time protected

HOW TO STEP INTO THE CEO ROLE

Here's what helped me evolve from being the "safety net" in my business to becoming a true CEO:

1. *Clarity:* I wrote a list of things I wanted to stop doing. Then I created SOPs or found people to own those areas.
2. *Hiring a COO/Integrator:* I brought someone in to take over day-to-day operations, allowing me to focus on vision and growth.

3. *Empowering the Leadership Team:* I stopped micro-managing and started mentoring. We implemented clear KPIs, structured meetings, and gave leaders real ownership.
4. *Systems:* We leaned on tech, AI, and automation to build a business that works even when I'm offline.
5. *CEO Time:* I block time every week for deep work, journalling, and big-picture thinking. It's non-negotiable.
6. *Hiring a Business Coach:* Everyone needs a coach. My coach helped me see my blind spots, challenged the beliefs that were keeping me stuck, and gave me tools to lead with confidence and clarity.

THE LEAP THAT FEELS IMPOSSIBLE

One of the biggest objections I hear from entrepreneurs is, *"I can't afford a COO or senior leadership team. Isn't that only for bigger businesses?"* I used to believe that too. When I had a team of over ten offshore staff, I thought I had great support. But the truth was, I was still the one coming up with all the ideas, executing with the help of the team, and cross checking every stage of the process.

I convinced myself I couldn't afford senior local staff, so I settled on being the only senior person in the company. Then one day, a friend who had just left her marketing job approached me about working together. My first reaction was, *"No way, I can't afford this."* But deep down I knew the truth: if I didn't start building leadership around me, I'd stay stuck in the weeds. So I took the leap. It was scary, and it took a few months before I saw the return on investment. But eventually, she took the Marketing hat off me and became our Head of Marketing.

Not long after, I had the opportunity to hire senior people in Sales and Operations. That was even scarier, it meant investing even more money, but I knew that to reach the next level I had to let go of more hats.

It was an expensive investment, but absolutely worth it for the freedom it created. The question you need to ask yourself is this: Do you want bigger profits while you're stuck doing everything, or are you willing to accept smaller profits in exchange for freedom, the ability to work when you want to, and the space to pursue other passions?

Here's the paradox: waiting until you feel "big enough" to justify leadership hires is what keeps you small.

Growth comes after you let go, not before.

And remember, this isn't just about having people on your payroll. Some large businesses still have founders drowning in daily tasks because they refuse to release control. Meanwhile, smaller companies can run like true enterprises when the founder chooses to lead instead of do, trusts people to own their lane, and builds systems that create accountability without micromanagement.

Becoming the CEO isn't about the size of your business. It's about the size of your leadership.

FINAL THOUGHTS

You didn't start your business to be chained to your desk or stuck in the weeds. You started it to create freedom, impact, and a better life; for you, your family, your team, and your community.

Becoming the CEO isn't about stepping back. It's about stepping up to your highest purpose in the business. It's about designing your role intentionally so you can lead the company to its next level without losing yourself in the process.

You already have what it takes. You just need to give yourself permission.

ACTION STEPS

1. **Create a "Not Me" List.**
   Write down 10 things you currently do that someone else could take over. Then take action to remove yourself from at least 3 of them.
2. **Schedule CEO Time.**
   Block out 2–3 hours per week for strategic thinking, reviewing metrics, or future planning. Treat it like your most important meeting.
3. **Define your CEO Scorecard.**
   What are the top 3 outcomes only you can drive this quarter? How will you measure them?
4. **Empower your next leader.**
   Whether it's your COO, EA, or a department head, pick someone to take on more ownership. Coach them. Trust them. Let them grow.

CHAPTER 5.5
Mastering Your Finances

Let's talk about something most people avoid: **money.**

Not just how to make more of it but how to heal your relationship with it. How to manage it with confidence. How to use it to create peace, choice, and purpose.

Because money isn't just a number.

It's your *energy.*
It's your *freedom.*
It's your *quality of life.*

I KNOW WHAT IT'S LIKE TO STRUGGLE.

There was a time when I had nothing. I was a single mum on Centrelink, government support, scraping by.

I remember clearly, there was a day I only had $20 left to put petrol in the car, and I prayed it would last the week. Back then, money felt heavy and full of fear. I was constantly in survival mode. But I also knew: this wasn't where my story would end. I wanted freedom; for myself, for my child, for our future. And I knew that the first step was working on my money mindset.

REWIRING MY MONEY MINDSET

As I began my personal growth journey, I discovered teachings that completely changed my relationship with money. *Randy Gage's Prosperity Laws* taught me that true wealth starts in the mind, not the bank.

It challenged me to act from an abundant mindset, even when it felt uncomfortable. *Ken Honda's Happy Money* showed me how to bring gratitude and joy into every financial exchange, whether giving or receiving.

And I also found *Leanne Jacobs' Beautiful Money*, who said:

> *"Wealth is not just about how much you earn, but how aligned, empowered, and conscious you are with your money."*

I learned that creating wealth doesn't have to feel like hustle, pressure, or stress. It can feel beautiful, calm, organised, and graceful. It's not just about spreadsheets and savings targets; it's about self-worth, boundaries, and how you value your time, energy, and gifts.

STEWARDSHIP: A SHIFT IN PERSPECTIVE

Something else I realised along the way is that money isn't something we truly control, it's something we are entrusted to take care of. We can't take it with us when we die. We are only managing it for the time we are alive.

Whether you believe in God, the universe, or simply doing good in the world, I found deep peace in seeing myself not as the owner of wealth, but as a *steward* of it.

It reminded me of the verses in the Bible: 1 Timothy 6:7, "For we brought nothing into the world, and we can take nothing out of it." And Luke 16:10, "Whoever can be trusted with very little can also be trusted with much."

I started asking myself:

1. *Am I managing what I have well?*
2. *Am I using my resources in a way that aligns with my values?*
3. *How can I be more intentional with the money I receive, earn, and give?*
4. *Am I holding on to money loosely, knowing it can come and go?*
5. *If money can't follow me when I die, how do I want it to speak for me while I live?*

When you manage money with purpose, whether it's $100 or $100,000, you start to feel more grounded, more generous, and more at peace. Money stops being a source of anxiety or pride, and becomes a tool for meaning, impact, and joy.

ABUNDANCE VS. LACK

I've met people who have built significant wealth and yet still live in lack. First, they feared not having enough. Then, after they built their fortune, they feared losing it. They hoard. They stress. They never truly feel "safe."

I've also met people with modest means who give freely, sleep peacefully, and carry themselves with a deep sense of abundance. Their joy isn't tied to the size of their bank account, it's tied to their trust that life will always provide what they need.

It's not just about how much you have. It's about how you relate to what you have.

An abundant money mindset says:

"There's always more where that came from."

"I trust money to flow in and out with purpose."

"My value is not tied to my bank account."

When you think abundantly, you stop gripping money so tightly. You start to see it as a resource that flows, a current that's meant to move through you, not something to be locked away in fear. This shift creates generosity, creativity, and peace of mind.

I remember learning this lesson from Randy Gage at the beginning of my personal development journey. He challenged me to practise giving even when it felt uncomfortable. At that time, I had only about $500 in my bank account, yet I chose to give $50 to charity. It felt risky, but I trusted the principle of circulation. That same week, I landed a new client and even found a $50 note tucked away in an old pair of jeans. It was my first real taste of the spiritual side of wealth, realising that money is more than just earning and saving. It is also about mindset and the energy we put out into the world. Are we sending out signals of abundance, or signals of lack? As Wayne Dyer said, *"Abundance is not something we acquire. It is something we tune into."* And as Proverbs 11:25 reminds us, *"A generous person will prosper; whoever refreshes others will be refreshed."*

Abundance isn't about clinging tightly to what you have, it's about trusting that there is always more, and that by giving freely, you create space to receive.

BUILDING LASTING WEALTH

So many entrepreneurs get caught up in building revenue but forget to build financial freedom. All their money is tied up in the business. They are asset rich but cash poor. And when business slows down, their whole life wobbles.

From the beginning, my husband and I shared one goal: Become debt free and build long term personal wealth. We used our income to invest in property, focused on paying off our mortgages, and lived within our means. Every time the business created profit, we looked for ways to turn it into real, lasting security.

Here are some guiding principles that helped us:

- ***Pay yourself first.*** Before reinvesting everything back into the business, set aside a portion for personal savings or investments.

- *Avoid lifestyle creep.* As income grows, it's tempting to upgrade cars, homes, or holidays. We were mindful about not spending more than we make.
- *Separate business and personal finances.* Your company might generate wealth, but your family security should not depend entirely on business cash flow.
- *Invest for the long term.* We focused on assets like property that grow steadily in value, generate passive income, and build long term equity.
- *Be intentional with debt.* Not all debt is bad, but we made it a priority to eliminate personal debt so that we had true freedom and flexibility.

I've seen too many entrepreneurs burn out chasing bigger revenue without building a safety net.

They live like millionaires on paper, but their peace of mind is fragile. Real wealth is quiet and it doesn't need to prove itself. It gives you the ability to sleep at night without worrying if one bad month in business will wipe you out.

PAY YOURSELF FIRST

One of the most important mindset shifts I ever made in business was learning to pay myself first and fairly.

Too often, I see business owners who pay themselves less than their executive assistant. They're making sales, growing the business, reinvesting every dollar... but forgetting one thing: *they're the one building it all.*

I used to do the same. Every time money came in, I'd pour it straight back into the business; new hires, new software, marketing campaigns and only pay myself if there was something left. Some months, that meant nothing. I told myself, *"This is what sacrifice looks like."*

But that kind of thinking creates burnout and resentment. If you're always the last to get paid, how long will you keep pouring into the business before you feel drained?

A book I recommend is *Profit First* by Mike Michalowicz. It teaches a powerful principle: prioritise profit and allocate that amount before paying any bills.

Even if you start with a small percentage, it's about building the habit, intentionally carving out profit before it fades away through more reinvestment. Over time, that small habit builds real financial stability.

The formula flips the traditional model:

- *Old way:* Income – Expenses = Profit
- *Profit First way:* Income – Profit = Expenses

This simple mindset shift changed how I ran my business. I no longer saw profit as "whatever's left over", I treated it as something I deserved and planned for.

If you're building a business that doesn't pay you well, you're not creating freedom; you're just building another job. My mentor, Steve, used to challenge me to increase my pay regularly, just like you would with your team. He believed that paying yourself well empowers you, motivates you, and removes resentment.

And the funny thing is when you commit to paying yourself more, you often rise to the occasion. You find a way. You earn more to support it.

THE BUCKET SYSTEM

Another game changing idea I learnt is the bucket system. It transformed the way I manage money both in business and life.

The idea is simple but powerful: give every dollar a job by allocating it into clearly defined accounts or "buckets."

This concept was taught to me from the *The Barefoot Investor* book which focuses on personal financial management and *Profit First* for managing your business finance.

When money flows in, it gets divided into purpose-driven accounts, so you always know what's safe to spend and what needs to be saved or reserved for later rather than having it sit all in one pot.

Before I discovered the bucket system, I had everything sitting in one account. Tax money, payroll, expenses, and my own income. I'd check the balance and think, *"Sweet, I've got money!"* So I'd spend it either on a new course, a marketing campaign, or general expenses.

But when it came time to pay the tax bill or do payroll, I was blindsided.

Sometimes, I didn't have enough not because the business wasn't making money, but because I hadn't allocated properly. The money wasn't really mine to spend. I just hadn't given it a name or a home.

Once I created separate accounts and gave every dollar a job, everything changed. I could instantly see what's safe to spend and what's growing quietly in the background.

Even during tight months, I felt calm. There was structure. There was clarity.

That's the power of the *bucket system.*

Here's what the business buckets look like in practice. You set up separate accounts, each with a clear purpose:

1. ***Revenue:*** All client payments flow into this account first.
2. ***Profit:*** Set aside for long-term savings and owner dividends.
3. ***Payroll:*** Covers your consistent take-home wage and the wages of your staff.
4. ***Tax:*** Covers BAS, super, and your tax obligations.
5. ***Operating Expenses:*** Everything required to run the business day to day.

Once revenue comes in, you divide it into these buckets based on present percentages tailored to your business.

This ensures you're always prepared and never caught off guard by tax time or cash flow dips.

The same approach works beautifully in your personal life. Here are the key buckets to set up:

- *Income:* Your salary or drawings land here first.
- *Everyday Expenses:* Essentials like rent, groceries, and bills.
- *Giving:* Money for giving to charity or church
- *Splurge:* Guilt-free money to spend on fun stuff.
- *Savings:* For big life goals like holidays or renovations.
- *Emergency:* Your emergency fund and peace-of-mind safety net.

As with business, your personal income gets split into these buckets automatically. The key is setting percentages that work for you and sticking to them.

If you want detailed guidance, I highly recommend reading *Profit First* and *The Barefoot Investor*. These books walk you through setup and allocation with practical examples that can change your financial future.

YOUR PERSONAL WEALTH SYSTEM

While paying myself first and using the bucket system helped to an extent, I realised I still lacked clarity on our financial position and where we were heading.

Early in our relationship, my husband and I would often disagree about money. Not because we were struggling, but because we were unsure if we were truly progressing. When you only measure money by the cash you spend, the cards you tap, or your bank balance, it's easy to feel lost. Then the bills roll in, and suddenly it feels like all your hard work and life savings are being drained. You start to question:

Why am I working so hard if the money disappears faster than I earn it?
Are we actually better or worse off than last year?
Are we paying down debt fast enough?
Is our wealth even growing?

These lingering questions create uncertainty. And ultimately, lack of clarity creates stress. To ease the tension and reduce money disagreements, I decided to treat our personal finances with the same seriousness I gave to the business.

I built a simple system using an Excel spreadsheet with multiple tabs to track everything, from our net worth, debt repayments, to cashflow report, so we could clearly see where we stood and where we were going. That clarity gave us shared peace of mind, better decision-making, and most importantly, helped justify why I could spend on holidays, something he still thinks I do a little too often!

Let me introduce you to some simple systems and templates that can help you create financial clarity and peace of mind for your family.

TEMPLATE 1: PERSONAL BALANCE SHEET OR NETWORTH TRACKER:

This is the first place to start. Think of it like stepping on the scales, it gives you a clear snapshot of where you're currently at financially.

Knowing your net worth helps you understand whether you're moving forward or falling behind over time.

Your net worth is calculated by subtracting what you owe (liabilities) from what you own (assets).

Here's how to do it:

Step 1: List all your assets
(things you own e.g. property, car, savings, super)

Step 2: List all your liabilities
(debts you owe e.g. mortgage, credit cards, loans)

Step 3: Subtract liabilities from assets
(this number is your current net worth)

Track your net worth every 6 or 12 months to see real progress. You'll gain visibility over whether you've reduced your liabilities and whether your assets have grown in value. Remember, what gets measured gets managed and this simple habit can help you make more intentional financial decisions.

Asset	Current Value	Notes
Home Property	$__________	(Estimate or bank valuation)
Investment Property 1	$__________	
Investment Property 2	$__________	
Cash Savings (Bank Accounts)	$__________	
Retirement Funds / Super	$__________	
Stocks / Shares	$__________	
Crypto / Other Investments	$__________	
Business Ownership (Est. Value)	$__________	
Cars (Market Value)	$__________	
Other Assets (e.g., collectibles)	$__________	

Liability	Outstanding Balance
Mortgage on Home	$__________
Mortgage on Investment Properties	$__________
Credit Card Debt	$__________
Personal Loans	$__________
Car Loans	$__________
Other Liabilities	$__________

Category	Amount
Total Assets	$__________
Total Liabilities	$__________
Net Worth (Assets – Liabilities)	$__________

TEMPLATE 2: CASHFLOW TRACKER

Once you know your net worth, the next step is understanding your cash flow.

This report gives you a clear picture of what's coming in, what's going out, and where your money is really going each month.

You might think you already know but most people are surprised when they see it all laid out. Tiny leaks in spending, forgotten subscriptions, or lifestyle creep can quietly drain your finances. But when you track it intentionally, you regain control.

This report is your personal profit and loss statement, helping you stay proactive, not reactive.

Step 1: Record your income by listing all the sources of money flowing in every month

Step 2: Record your expenses by listing every major spending category and the approximate amount you spend in each area monthly. (If you're unsure, check your bank/credit card statements from the past 3 months.)

Step 3: Calculate your totals by adding up your total income and total expenses.

Step 4: Find your monthly surplus or deficit, then subtract your total expenses from your total income.

Step 5: Track trends over time and complete a new report monthly or quarterly to spot patterns, adjust, and stay proactive.

Step 6: Make better financial decisions by using your reports to decide when you can: take a holiday, invest in assets, save for future goals, cut down unnecessary spending and feel in control, not reactive.

Income Source	**Monthly Amount**
Business Income	$_________
Salary / Wages	$_________
Rental Income	$_________
Dividends / Investment Income	$_________
Other Income (e.g. side gigs)	$_________
Other Income	$_________

Expense Category	**Monthly Amount**
Mortgage / Rent	$_________
Utilities (Electricity, Gas, Water)	$_________
Phone & Internet	$_________
Groceries	$_________
Dining Out / Coffee	$_________

Transportation (Fuel, Car, Train)	$__________
Insurance (Home, Health, Car)	$__________
Subscriptions (Netflix, Spotify, etc.)	$__________
Health & Fitness (Gym, Health Apps)	$__________
Kids' Expenses (School, Activities)	$__________
Personal Spending (Clothing, Beauty)	$__________
Gifts & Charity	$__________
Travel / Holidays	$__________
Business Expenses	$__________
Other Expenses	

Category	**Amount**
Total Income	$__________
Total Expenses	$__________
Monthly Surplus/Deficit (Income – Expenses)	$__________

TEMPLATE 3: THE BARE MINIMUM LIVING EXPENSES

Life is full of surprises, some beautiful, some challenging. Whether it's a slow business season, a job loss, or an unexpected life event, knowing your survival number (your bare minimum monthly expenses) can give you peace of mind and a solid plan when things get tight.

This template helps you calculate the absolute minimum you need each month to keep the lights on, food on the table, and your family secure. It's not about scarcity, it's about safety. When you know your floor, you remove panic from the equation and replace it with calm, confident decision-making.

Here's how to calculate it:

Step 1: Strip it back.

Using your Expense Tracking template above, remove all non-essential costs: (No Netflix, no dining out, no luxury extras, only true necessities like housing, groceries, insurance, and basic transport.)

Step 2: Use it for smart planning.

- Set emergency fund goals
- Plan for business slow seasons
- Map out your retirement runway

Step 3: Review it yearly.

As life changes (kids grow, mortgages shift, new stages happen), your minimum number will change too, so keep it updated.

TEMPLATE 4. WAR CHEST EXERCISE

In ancient times, kings and generals kept a war chest, a physical box filled with gold, weapons, and supplies, tucked away for moments of crisis or opportunity. It wasn't touched for everyday life. It was a lifeline. A strategic reserve to survive sieges, win unexpected battles, or strike at the perfect moment. In modern life and business, we need the same kind of buffer.

Your war chest is your personal and business financial defence system. It's not for paying bills or funding day-to-day expenses. It's a protected stash designed to help you weather storms, ride out downturns, or take advantage of unexpected opportunities with confidence instead of fear.

When your war chest is in place, you feel unshakeable. You're not making decisions from stress or survival, you're operating from strength and strategy.

Step 1: Calculate Your Baseline Needs

Start by figuring out what it would take to keep things afloat if everything stopped tomorrow.

- Personal: Add up your essential monthly living costs.
- Business: Add up your non-negotiable monthly business costs.

Step 2: Set Your War Chest Goal

Once you've got your monthly essentials figured out, calculate the full war chest amount by multiplying the baseline by 3 or 6 months. For example:

> $10,000/month essential living expenses × 6 months = $60,000
>
> $100,000/month essential business expenses × 3 months = $300,000
>
> Total War Chest Goal = $360,000

This becomes your target to work toward.

Step 3: Separate Your War Chest from Daily Money

This step is key: do not mix your war chest with everyday money.

Create a separate high-interest savings account, offset account, or business savings account. Label it clearly as "War Chest". This is not "just in case" money for casual use. It's protected, strategic capital.

Out of sight, out of mind, but always ready when it matters most.

Step 4: Build It Monthly (Without Feeling the Pinch)

Start feeding your war chest gradually and consistently. Here are a few ways:

- Set aside 10–20% of your monthly business profit
- Allocate a portion of your salary or drawings
- Redirect tax refunds, bonuses, or windfalls
- Use side hustle income
- Channel dividends or investment income

Small, steady contributions compound fast especially when you're intentional about it.

Category	Target Amount	Notes
Emergency Fund (3–6 months essential expenses)	$_________	Bare minimum living costs (multiply 3-6)
Business Buffer (3–6 months fixed costs)	$_________	Office, staff salaries, software, etc.
Total War Chest Goal	$_________	

TEMPLATE 5: PERSONAL FINANCIAL GOAL TEMPLATE

This template is here to help you set clear, meaningful financial goals that aren't just about stacking more money. Without clear goals, it's easy to fall into the trap of working harder, earning more, but still feeling stressed and stuck. Real financial freedom isn't just about how much you make, it's about how intentionally you use, grow, and protect what you have.

Step 1: Define Your Big Vision

Question	Your Answer
What does financial freedom mean to you?	
How much passive income would make you feel secure?	$__________/month
When would you like to achieve it by?	__________(date)

Step 2: Personal Income Goals

Goal	Amount	Notes
Annual Personal Income Target	$__________	Salary + business draw
Monthly Personal Income Target	$__________	Annual Income ÷ 12
Other Income Streams Target (Rental, Dividends, etc.)	$__________ / month	

Step 3: Savings Goals

Goal	Amount	Notes
Emergency Fund (3–6 months living expenses)	$__________	(E.g., by Dec 2025)
Holiday Fund	$__________	

Big Purchase (Car, Home, Wedding)	$__________	
Other Savings Goals	$__________	

Step 4: Investment Goals

Goal	Target Amount	Notes
Property Investment	$__________	(Deposit or lump sum)
Share Portfolio	$__________	(E.g., ETFs, managed funds)
Superannuation Boost	$__________	(Additional voluntary contributions)
Other Investments (Business, Crypto, etc.)	$__________	

Step 5: Debt Reduction Goals

Debt Type	Current Balance	Goal Payoff Date
Credit Card 1	$__________	
Personal Loan	$__________	
Mortgage Extra Repayments	$__________	
Other Debts	$__________	

PAYING ON TIME

One of the biggest sources of hidden stress for entrepreneurs is falling behind on payments whether it's bills, loan repayments, subscriptions, or tax.

It may seem manageable at first, but delaying payments can quickly snowball into late fees, anxiety, and a feeling of being constantly behind. But there's a better way. Paying on time is more than just good business practice, it's a mindset.

It's a way to stay in integrity, reduce financial stress, and build a peaceful relationship with money.

In *Happy Money,* Ken Honda talks about paying bills with grace, thanking the person or company for the value they've provided and releasing money with appreciation instead of resentment. That includes your electricity provider, accountant, software platforms, and yes, even the government.

It's not always easy to enjoy paying bills, but here's a perspective shift that helped me: If you have bills to pay, it means you're alive, you're using services, and you're earning.

Your money isn't being thrown away in the bin, it's helping someone else get paid, run their business, or serve others. You're part of the flow.

Here are a few simple ways to stay on top of payments:

- Use payment plans if needed; spreading costs out can remove pressure without falling behind
- Set up direct debits for recurring bills so they're handled automatically

- Create separate buckets/accounts for future bills, so the money is ready when needed
- Track due dates in your calendar and review upcoming payments weekly to stay ahead

When you pay with intention, you stay in control and peace replaces pressure. Because nothing feels better than knowing your bills are covered, your mind is clear, and you're not being chased. You're leading with calm confidence!

FINAL THOUGHTS

You don't have to wait until you "make it" to feel financially free. You can start right now, with the mindset, systems, and habits that support you. History is full of stories of people who earned more money than most of us could imagine—yet lost it all. Mike Tyson earned over $400 million in his boxing career but declared bankruptcy.

Michael Jackson made hundreds of millions through music and touring but left behind hundreds of millions in debt. Their downfall wasn't because they couldn't make money, it was because they didn't manage it well.

Financial freedom isn't about how much you can earn, it's about how wisely you manage what flows through your hands. You can be the kind of person who:

- *Earns with alignment*
- *Spends with joy*
- *Saves with purpose*
- *Gives with love*

Because true wealth is how you feel, not just what you have. And when your financial world becomes peaceful, intentional, and beautiful, everything else flows better too.

"Money is a tool. Freedom is the goal. Live intentionally, not reactively."

ACTION STEPS

1. Read Beautiful Money, Profit First, or Happy Money; start wherever your heart feels called.
2. Reflect: What beliefs about money are you still carrying and are they helping or hurting?
3. Review the financial templates and complete them.
4. Choose one area to make your money feel more beautiful; clear out old bills, create a giving plan, or write affirmations around abundance.

Section 6: The Business of Happiness

"The goal is not more money. The goal is living life on your terms." — Chris Brogan

CHAPTER 6.1

How to Measure Fulfilment, Not Just Revenue

As entrepreneurs, we've mastered the art of measuring business performance. We track revenue, profit margins, KPIs, and growth percentages like second nature. But when it comes to measuring our personal fulfilment, our joy, peace, and sense of purpose, we're often flying blind.

What if you treated your happiness the same way you treat your business?

What if you applied the same level of discipline and clarity to your inner life as you do to your bottom line?

Many entrepreneurs convince themselves that burnout is just part of the journey. That joy can wait.

That they'll be happy "when..." But postponing fulfilment is like running a business that reinvests everything and never pays a dividend.

What's the point of all the effort if you never get to feel alive? In fact, research from Harvard and Yale shows that happiness fuels higher productivity, better decision-making, and stronger resilience. Fulfilment is not just a fluffy bonus, it's a smart strategy.

It makes your success more sustainable, your leadership more impactful, and your life more worthwhile. Let's reframe how you think about happiness by borrowing a concept from business: The Fulfilment Profit & Loss Statement (P&L)

THE FULFILMENT P&L STATEMENT

In business, a P&L shows the income and expenses over a set period, revealing whether you're running at a profit or a loss. Your Fulfilment P&L does the same for your life. It tracks what energises you (fulfilment income) and what drains you (fulfilment expenses) week to week. It gives you a clear picture of whether your life is emotionally profitable, not just financially successful.

Ask yourself: *What's pouring into your energy bank, and what's quietly draining it?*

Fulfilment Income

These are the life-giving activities that fill your cup and bring you back to balance:

- Quality time spent with loved ones each week
- Hours spent on work that brings meaning or joy
- Hours spent exercising and moving your body

- Daily moments of gratitude, prayer, or spiritual connection
- Number of healthy meals that fuelled your body and mind

Fulfilment Expenses

These are the energy drains that chip away at your well-being, often unnoticed:

- Hours spent in purposeless meetings or draining conversations
- Time on tasks that feel misaligned with your strengths or values
- Interactions with people who zap your energy
- Hours lost doom scrolling or on mindless screen time
- Days lost to hangovers or low moods from drinking

HOW TO TRACK YOUR FULFILMENT

If you're serious about increasing fulfilment, treat it with the same rigour as your business metrics.

1. Use "Emotional Units"

Assign simple values to activities based on how they impact your energy and emotions:

+100 = Deep joy (e.g. family holiday, spiritual retreat)
+50 = Rejuvenating (e.g. quality time, exercise)
-50 = Minor drain (e.g. admin task)
-100 = Energy zapper (e.g. toxic interaction, burnout)

2. Set KPIs for Happiness

Just like you track sales and profit, track your joy.

Weekly KPIs: 3 workouts, 2 family dinners, 1 creative session

Monthly KPIs: 1 mini getaway, 4 friend catchups

Quarterly KPIs: 1 growth experience (e.g. course, retreat)

3. Build in Accountability

You hit goals faster with accountability, apply this to life too.

- Share your fulfilment KPIs with your assistant, coach, or accountability buddy
- Use a weekly scorecard or Google Sheet to track progress
- Celebrate your wins monthly, note your biggest fulfilment "dividend"

Your Fulfilment Statement Example

YOU INC.

FULFILMENT STATEMENT

For the Year Ended Today (In Emotional Units)

JOYFUL ACTIVITIES

Time with family & friends 1,200

Purposeful work 950

Spiritual connection 650

Travel & new experiences 400

TOTAL FULFILMENT INCOME 3,200

ENERGY DRAINS

Overwork & burnout 800

Toxic relationships 500

Unaligned tasks 350

Screen time & comparison 250

TOTAL EXPENSES 1,900

NET FULFILMENT 1,300

Remember, your Fulfilment P&L is your emotional dashboard. Are you operating in surplus or living in the red?

FINAL THOUGHTS

Most of us started our business to make money, but not just for the sake of money. Deep down, we believed that financial success would bring fulfilment and happiness. If happiness is the true goal, then it makes sense to aim for it first and reverse engineer everything else around it.

Here's the truth: happiness isn't something you finally reach once you hit a number or achieve a milestone.

That kind of happiness is temporary. The real joy is found in the journey, in how you live, lead, and love along the way. When you are happy, you are more motivated, more creative, and you enjoy the process so much more.

The key is this: when you start measuring happiness and fulfilment with the same seriousness as revenue, everything changes.

You begin to honour your time, protect your energy, and prioritise what truly matters. You make better decisions not just for your business, but for your life.

The pursuit of happiness isn't just a dream, it is your responsibility as a leader.

Entrepreneurs who live in alignment with their values and intentionally build joy into their weeks are more resilient and ultimately more successful.

So don't wait for the future to feel alive. Build systems for joy now. Because happiness is the real ROI.

ACTION STEPS

1. Reflect on your Fulfilment P&L: What's filling your cup, and what's draining it?
2. Assign emotional units to your weekly routines.
3. Set one weekly and one monthly fulfilment KPI.
4. Schedule a quarterly check-in to review your life's "emotional profit"
5. Rinse and repeat.

CHAPTER 6.2

The Paradoxes for Success

Have you ever read a quote that hits you like a rock, where your brain just goes BOOM? That's what paradox quotes do to me.

I first stumbled across a collection of paradoxes in an online article on Farnam Street titled *"The Paradoxes of Life."* A paradox is a statement that seems contradictory at first glance, but holds a deeper truth beneath the surface.

These quotes are often short and simple, yet they have the power to completely shift your perspective.

They challenge what we've been conditioned to believe and remind us that, sometimes, doing the opposite of what feels logical is what actually works. These aren't just clever ideas, they're truths I've experienced first-hand. Below are five paradoxes that have the potential to transform how you approach business, leadership, and life.

1. THE SPEED PARADOX

"Slow down to speed up."

This paradox suggests that to achieve success faster, you actually need to slow down.

It feels counter-intuitive, especially when your to-do list is bursting, targets are looming, and people are counting on you. But staying in constant motion often means you're reacting, not intentionally leading. You might be sprinting... in the wrong direction.

When you're always in "go" mode, you lose the ability to zoom out and see the bigger picture. You climb fast, but sometimes realise too late that it was the wrong ladder all along. Slowing down gives you the space to think clearly, make better decisions, and align your actions with what truly matters.

That's often when the real breakthroughs come.

I remember one day feeling stuck on a big decision. Instead of forcing it at my desk, I went for a walk. On that walk, I randomly bumped into someone who later became a client, and eventually, a strategic partner.

That simple pause led to more progress than hours of grinding would have. Hustle might move you quickly. But clarity is what ensures you're actually headed in the right direction.

2. THE PRODUCTIVITY PARADOX

"Work more, achieve less."

This paradox reminds us that working more hours doesn't necessarily lead to more results. In fact, it often leads to the opposite; burnout, mistakes, and missed opportunities.

Entrepreneurs often convince themselves, *"If I just work one more hour, I'll get ahead."* But that extra hour is usually filled with half-focus; staring at a screen, rereading emails, or doing low-impact tasks that feel like progress but aren't. I've been guilty of this too, putting in long hours only to feel like I barely moved the needle. My energy drained, my creativity dried up, and simple tasks stretched unnecessarily.

That's where Parkinson's Law hits home: *work expands to fill the time you give it.* If you allow a task to take all day, it will. So I started working like a lion. Lions don't graze all day like cows, they hunt in short, powerful bursts. Then they rest. Then they strike again.

I began setting tight windows for focused work and gave myself real breaks in between.

The result? Higher output, better decisions, and way more energy left for life. Work like a lion: sprint with focus, then rest with intention. That's how real productivity happens.

3. THE SAY NO PARADOX

"Take on less, accomplish more."

This paradox is a powerful reminder that saying no is not a weakness, it's a strength. In fact, the more you say no, the more space you create to say yes to what truly matters. This was one of the hardest lessons I had to learn. For years, I said yes to everything.

Every opportunity, every collaboration, every invite.

I did not want to miss out. I was scared that *this* could be the big break, the game-changer, the thing that would take me to the next level. But here's what really happened: I got stretched thin.

The more I said yes, the less energy I had for the things that actually mattered; my vision, my health, my family. I was constantly busy but rarely fulfilled. Productive but not purposeful.

I started to notice something about the most successful and peaceful people I admired, they weren't just smart. They were *selective*. They didn't let FOMO (fear of missing out) dictate their decisions. They didn't apologise for protecting their time.

I realised: *Every yes is a no to something else.* Saying yes to every podcast invite, every lunch meeting, every low-priority project, was saying no to writing my book or going for a walk with my kids after school.

Now, I guard my calendar like it's sacred. I plan life before work. I have a system to help me pause before I commit my "Maybe List."

If I'm unsure, I write it down and revisit it a week later. Nine times out of ten, what once felt urgent no longer feels important. And I save myself from commitments that drain instead of energise.

Saying no isn't about being rude or selfish, it's about being clear. It's about protecting your highest priorities so they don't get buried under someone else's.

As Derek Sivers said: *"If it's not a hell yes, it's a no."* And I've learned that saying no to the wrong things is what creates space for the right things to flourish.

4. THE CONNECTEDNESS PARADOX

"More connected than ever, yet more disconnected than ever."

This paradox means that despite being constantly plugged in through phones, social media, and messaging apps... we're often lacking the depth of connection that truly fulfils us.

We're surrounded by communication, but starving for genuine connection. In today's world, we can reach anyone at any time. We have hundreds of "friends," dozens of group chats, and instant notifications from across the globe.

But despite being more digitally connected than any generation before us, many people report feeling lonelier, more distracted, and emotionally distant from themselves and from those closest to them.

We scroll through perfectly curated lives on social media while sitting next to loved ones without making eye contact. We respond to work emails at the dinner table. We check messages out of habit, not intention. The result? Our relationships suffer not just with others, but with ourselves.

I had to learn this the hard way. I was replying to emails on holidays, checking messages in bed, and bringing my phone to every meal. It seemed harmless, but it left me feeling constantly "on" yet strangely disconnected. I wasn't truly present.

Now, I set boundaries: No phones at the dinner table. No work-related notifications after 8pm and I leave my phone in another room during bed time. It's not about being anti-technology, it's about being pro-presence. Because true connection doesn't come from being constantly reachable, it comes from being fully present. From undistracted eye contact. From deep conversations. From putting the phone down and really listening. That's where the real connection lives.

5. THE CONTROL PARADOX

"More controlling, less control."

This paradox means that the more tightly you try to control everything e.g. people, outcomes, timelines, the more things seem to slip through your fingers. True control often comes from letting go, trusting others, and focusing only on what's truly within your power.

Letting go is hard, especially when something feels deeply personal. Whether it's business, parenting, or relationships, we often cling tighter, thinking control equals safety, stability, or success. But here's the truth I've come to learn: The more you try to control, the more you push people away. I know this because I experienced it first-hand growing up.

My parents were incredibly strict. Their way of showing love was through control. Controlling where I went, what I wore, who I spoke to and what I believed. They wanted the best for me, but it didn't feel like love. It felt like a prison.

And so, I rebelled. I ran away. I rejected their rules and for a long time, I rejected them too. The more they tried to hold on, the more I pulled away. The more they controlled, the less control they had.

That experience shaped how I show up today as a mother, a wife, a leader. It taught me that freedom and trust are more powerful than control. Now as a business owner, I constantly remind myself not to repeat the same pattern with my team.

When I used to hover and try to fix things before they even had a chance, I noticed the same resistance forming. But when I stepped back, offering guidance, trust, and autonomy, they rose to the challenge. They made decisions. They owned outcomes. And more often than not, they exceeded my expectations.

The same applies to every relationship in our lives. Whether it's your child, your partner, or your staff, trying to control them only creates disconnection.

You think you're protecting the outcome, but you're actually limiting the potential. Letting go doesn't mean you stop caring. It means you trust enough to create space for others to grow.

Here's what I've learned:

- Set clear boundaries and expectations, then allow space.
- Lead with guidance, not fear.
- Support people through their mistakes instead of preventing them.
- Celebrate autonomy, even if the path looks different than yours.

Control might feel like love but it often breeds rebellion. Trust is what builds connection, confidence, and true leadership.

FINAL THOUGHTS

These paradoxes aren't just catchy sayings, they're counter-intuitive truths that can radically shift the way you live and lead.

Each one invites you to question the default and lean into what actually creates fulfilment.

- *Slow down to speed up:* Rest, reflect, and realign so you can move with clarity and purpose not just momentum.
- *Work more, achieve less:* Shorten your hours, sharpen your focus, and watch your creativity soar.
- *Take on less, accomplish more:* Your time is limited, guard it fiercely and give it only to what truly matters.
- *More connected than ever, yet more disconnected than ever:* Step away from the noise to be fully present with the people and moments that fuel you. Disconnect to truly connect.
- *More controlling, less control:* Empower others, release the need to micromanage, and trust that freedom builds stronger outcomes. Let go to gain real control.

In a world addicted to urgency, you get to choose intentionality.

ACTION STEPS

1. **Sprint like a lion:** Try focused 90-minute work blocks with intentional rest of 15 minutes, download a focus app like Focus Friend to help you keep yourself accountable.
2. **Delegate with trust:** Let go of one task you've been micromanaging, watch your team rise.
3. **Reconnect meaningfully:** Have one tech-free conversation or meal with a loved one this week.

CHAPTER 6.3

Life Audit – Performance Managing Your Life

In business, we hold performance reviews, track KPIs, and adjust strategy based on what's working and what's not.

We set clear goals and timelines, and we check in often. But when it comes to our personal lives, the stuff that truly matters, we tend to leave it to chance. We drift. We say we'll "get around to it."

And before we know it, another quarter, another year has passed, and we're wondering why we feel unfulfilled, off-balance, or stuck in the same habits.

What if we managed our lives with the same clarity and intention we bring to our businesses? I first learned about the power of a personal "life audit" during a session with my life coach, Uma Panch.

She had me reflect deeply on the different areas of my life, not just business, my health, family, marriage, self-care, and more. While the categories she used were slightly different to the ones I share in this book, the principle was the same: check in with yourself intentionally and regularly, just like you would in a business review.

That process was eye-opening. It made me realise that although my business was thriving on the outside, other areas of my life weren't getting the same level of attention or strategy.

I was running fast, but I wasn't necessarily aligned.

Since then, I've adopted this practice as a regular ritual. It helps me stay honest with myself, catch imbalances before they spiral, and make small course corrections that create a big difference over time.

THE 5 PILLARS OF 360° SUCCESS AUDIT

Just like in business, you can't improve what you don't measure. A life audit helps you:

- Spot the gaps between where you are and where you want to be
- Get honest about how fulfilled you actually feel (not just how productive you are)
- Create specific and aligned goals that actually matter
- Reclaim power in areas that feel stuck or neglected

In *The 7 Habits of Highly Effective People,* Stephen Covey encourages us to "begin with the end in mind." A life audit helps you do exactly that, by identifying what a 10/10 life looks like *for you,* and where you are today.

Here's how I like to assess where I'm at in life. Using the 5 Pillars of 360° Success, I reflect and score myself honestly from 1 to 10 in each area.

I ask myself two key questions:

1. *What does a 10/10 look like for me in this pillar?*
2. *Where am I right now, honestly, on a scale from 1 to 10?*

EXAMPLE LIFE AUDIT

My 5 Pillars	What 10/10 Looks Like For Me	My Current Score
Empowered Connection	*I feel deeply connected to my friends and regularly spend meaningful time with them. I add value to the people and community around me*	7
Business Freedom	*My business runs without me. I do what I love, can take time off freely, and never stress about money.*	8

Self-Mastery	*I invest in my health, discipline my mind, walk closely with God, and live from a place of peace and purpose.*	9
Family Balance	*I am fully present with my kids, enjoy quality time with them, and have a happy, passionate marriage.*	7
Life Experiences	*I intentionally create joy, take holidays, laugh often, unplug from work, and feel truly alive.*	9

Once I've defined what a 10/10 looks like and assessed my current score, I look at the gap and ask myself: *What's the one thing or habit I can do to move closer to a 10?*

It's not about making a giant leap overnight, it's about small shifts, one habit, one commitment, one calendar block at a time.

Here are some ideas I have listed out to bridge the gap between my current score and my ideal 10.

Empowered Connection

Action for improvement: Reach out to one friend this week just to connect, no agenda. Set a reminder to check in with 1 person per week.

Business Freedom

Action for improvement: Block two hours this week to delegate tasks that I shouldn't be doing. Set a reminder to audit my time every 3 months.

Self-Mastery

Action for improvement: Set a daily alarm to do a 10-minute morning walk without my phone to clear my mind and connect with God.

Family Balance

Action for improvement: Each night before bed, thank my husband and kids for one specific thing they did that day.

Life Experiences

Action for improvement: Visit at least 2 new cities a year and tick off at least 2 items from my bucket list.

These are real-life examples from my own journey, areas I'm actively working on. Your scores will likely look different, and that's perfectly normal. What you choose to prioritise will depend on the unique season and circumstances of your life. How you spend your time and money is completely up to you.

If visiting two new cities sounds like an amazing dream but feels out of reach right now, why not set a goal to explore two new hiking spots in your state? It does not have to cost a lot of money. When I first started doing this, my goal was simply to travel once or twice a year. Over time, I evolved, and now I aim to travel somewhere once a month.

The key thing is don't compare your scores with anyone else. This is your life, your path, your priorities. The goal isn't to judge yourself or feel bad. It's simply to get clear.

To know where you are so you can make intentional shifts toward where you want to be. Even when you're scoring high, there's always room to grow.

And if you're scoring low in an area, it doesn't mean you're failing it just means it needs attention. Don't beat yourself up. Get curious, not critical. I recommend doing a life audit every 6 months.

Set a recurring reminder in your calendar. And if you need support to reflect honestly or create an action plan, don't hesitate to get professional help whether that's a coach, mentor, or therapist. Sometimes we can't see our own blind spots, and that's okay. What matters is being committed to realignment.

50 HABITS TO IMPROVE ALL AREAS OF YOUR LIFE

Here is a list designed to help you take practical, repeatable action across the five pillars of 360° Success. They are small, consistent actions that move you closer to a 10/10 life.

Each habit includes a clear timing or frequency, making it easy to integrate into your routine. Start by choosing one or two habits that resonate with you, and focus on building consistency.

Over time, these small but intentional actions will create powerful momentum across your relationships, business, health, family, and personal joy.

Empowered Connection

1. Send one message every Monday to reconnect with a friend
2. Organise an in person coffee or lunch to get to know someone every second Friday

3. Give one person a compliment before 12pm each day
4. Write and send a thank-you letter to someone every fortnight
5. Have one phone-free meal with a friend or family member each week
6. Attend one community or networking event per month
7. Do one unexpected kind gesture every week e.g. write a Linkedin recommendation without being asked or write a Google review for a business you've used recently.
8. Follow up with someone from your past every fortnight
9. Celebrate someone's win every Friday via message or call
10. Update and act on your 'connection list' every first Monday of the month

Business Freedom

1. Identify one low-value task you can delegate to your team every week.
2. Do a 30-minute time audit on the 1st of every month
3. Block out 2 hours of 'deep work' time daily (no interruptions)
4. Automate one system or tool each quarter

5. Document one Standard Operating Procedure (SOP) every two weeks
6. Batch all meetings on Tuesdays and Thursdays only
7. Schedule 1 hour of CEO thinking time every Friday morning
8. Read one business book a month
9. Turn off all notifications during 9am–12pm work hours daily
10. Conduct a 15-minute weekly review every Sunday evening

Self-Mastery

1. Wake up at the same time every day.
2. Do a 10-minute walk without your phone every morning
3. Journal for 10 minutes each night before bed
4. Write down 3 things you're grateful for every morning
5. Drink a full glass of water within 10 minutes of waking up
6. Meditate or pray for 10 minutes every morning after waking
7. Set a 30-minute daily window for social media (and stick to it)
8. Read 10 pages of a book or listen to a personal development podcast each day

9. Plan your meals every Sunday evening for the week ahead
10. Put your phone outside the bedroom every night by 9pm

Family Balance

1. Create a phone-free window from 6pm–8pm every evening
2. Plan and enjoy a family night every Friday (games, movie, outing)
3. Send a message of appreciation to your partner every Monday
4. Take each child on a one-on-one outing every month
5. Give your partner and kids a hug first thing in the morning and before bed
6. Say "thank you" to each family member at dinner every night
7. Do one household task together with your partner or kids each Sunday
8. Book a holiday with your partner (no kids) once a year
9. Schedule a date night every second Saturday
10. Ask each family member one meaningful question at dinner daily

Life Experiences

1. Schedule a 2-hour "joy block" in your calendar every Sunday
2. Try a new experience (class, hobby, food) every month
3. Plan your next holiday on the first weekend of every quarter
4. Say yes to one spontaneous outing every week
5. Write down 3 things that brought you joy each Friday
6. Tick one item off your bucket list every quarter
7. Take one full day off (no work, no screens) every week
8. Visit a new place (even local) every month
9. Dance or sing for 5 minutes every morning while getting ready
10. Book one fun event or experience at the start of every month

There are countless ways to optimise your life, you just need to take action and turn it into a habit. Don't wait for motivation.

Don't wait until your marriage is on the brink, you've burnt out, or life forces you to pay attention. Start now. Small steps today prevent big regrets tomorrow.

FINAL THOUGHTS

You are the CEO of your life.

But unlike business, there are no board meetings or annual reviews to hold you accountable to your happiness.

A business that ignores its performance data eventually breaks down. The same is true for life. Check in. Re-align. Adjust. You must decide what success looks like. You must commit to performance-managing your own fulfilment.

Because when life is aligned, business becomes lighter, more joyful, and more sustainable.

ACTION STEPS

1. Take the free quiz at linhpodetti.com to spot which of the Five Pillars need attention.
2. Review the list of 50 habits and choose one new habit for this month. Practise it daily until it feels natural, then add the next.
3. Add a recurring calendar reminder to review your life audit every six months.

Section 7: Linh's Life System

"Life is a system of systems — every choice, habit, and relationship feeds into the whole." — Unknown

CHAPTER 7.1

The S3C Method - A Life System That Works

Most entrepreneurs chase happiness without a framework. We optimise for business, hustle for financial success, and hope that happiness will eventually catch up.

But just like a thriving business needs systems, structure, and a strategic plan, so does a fulfilling life. That's where my personal life system comes in, one that has radically transformed how I live, lead, and show up every day. I first discovered this system when members of EO Melbourne, a group of established entrepreneurs, reached out to me. They told me how much they admired the way I live my life.

They noticed I created space for family, self-care, and fun while still running a growing business. Instead of filling the free time I gained from hiring staff and putting systems in place with more work, I protected that space and used it for the things that truly matter in life.

They asked if I would come and teach them how I do it. I was surprised by the request, but I said yes. With that speaking opportunity ahead, I sat down and began to dissect my life.

I reverse engineered what had felt instinctive for years. I looked at the work I had done with my life coach, the habits I had built, the mindset shifts I had made, and the systems I had put in place. What emerged was a clear method that had taken me years to master, but my goal is to help you shorten that journey to months.

It was a method I had been following instinctively, one that took me from chaos to clarity, from a life that felt "meh" to one that feels deeply fulfilling.

I now call it **Linh's Life System,** a name my friend Jacob from EO Singapore suggested (thanks Jacob, I owe you one). At its core are four ingredients: Self-Worth, Clarity, Consistency, and Calm. Together, they form what I call the S3C Method.

It is a holistic operating system for achieving sustainable success. These four elements build on each other and are meant to be strengthened in this exact order.

When they work together, you are not just productive, you are purposeful. You are not just achieving, you are aligned. Let's unpack each one.

S – SELF-WORTH

True happiness begins with how you see yourself.

> *"Self-worth is the internal sense of being good enough and worthy of love and belonging from others."*
> *— Psychology Today*

Self-worth changes everything and impacts everything you do. Because until we believe in our worth from within, no amount of external success will ever feel satisfying. If we want to live a truly fulfilling 360° life, we must stop chasing approval and start healing the beliefs that say we're not enough.

This part of the system, requires alot of work, alot of healing, but it's the most impactful work we will ever do. We'll go much deeper into this in the next chapter, where I'll share the full story of how I began healing my self-worth and how you can, too.

C – CLARITY

You can't build a joyful, meaningful life if you don't know what joy and meaning actually look like for you. We often say things like, *"I just want more balance,"* or *"I want to be more present."* But what does that really mean? What does it look like in your everyday life?

Clarity is about turning vague desires into clear definitions. It's about getting honest with yourself about what matters most, what no longer fits, and what kind of life you want to design from this point forward. Clarity isn't just about goals. It's about *identity.* When you know who you are and what you stand for, you make better decisions. You stop chasing what's shiny and start building what's true.

We've already covered clarity practices in Section 2 of this book, and we'll explore them even further in Chapter 7.3, where we dive deeper into how to build clarity into your identity, decision-making, and leadership.

C – CONSISTENCY

Success doesn't come from doing something once. It comes from doing it *again and again.* From showing up, not just when you feel like it, but especially when you don't. Anyone can show up on a good day.

When energy is high, motivation is strong, and everything's flowing, consistency is easy. But real growth happens on the days you don't feel like it. It's built in the mundane, in the *repeated,* in the *unseen.* That's where momentum lives.

Consistency isn't about doing everything perfectly. It's about showing up, again and again, for the things that truly matter. It's about becoming someone your future self can count on.

You don't need more willpower. You need better systems. When you build your life around aligned habits and anchored routines, success becomes a byproduct, not a push. We've already covered tools and habits for building consistency in Sections 3 & 4, but we'll explore it even further in Chapter 7.4, where we dive deeper into how to stay consistent when life gets messy.

C – CALM

Even with clarity and consistency, life will still throw you curveballs.

Storms will come.
Plans will change.
Unexpected challenges will test you.
That's why *calm* is essential.

Calm is what keeps you grounded when chaos hits. It's the difference between reacting out of fear and responding with wisdom and intention.

Calm isn't about living a stress-free life. That's not realistic. It's about having the tools, habits, and mindset to *navigate* stress with grace, resilience, and faith.

When we don't know how to manage our thoughts, shift our perspective, or use the tools available to support us, life can quickly spiral off track. We get caught in reactivity, anxiety, and overwhelm, losing sight of what matters most.

We've already explored practical calm-creating tools in Section 3 like morning routines, setting boundaries, and creating space as well as the powerful paradoxes in Chapter

6.2 that help you flow with life more gracefully. In Chapter 7.5, we'll explore even deeper how to anchor yourself in calm even when life feels unpredictable. These are all part of building your inner calm muscle.

HOW THIS MODEL WORKS – A HEALTH EXAMPLE

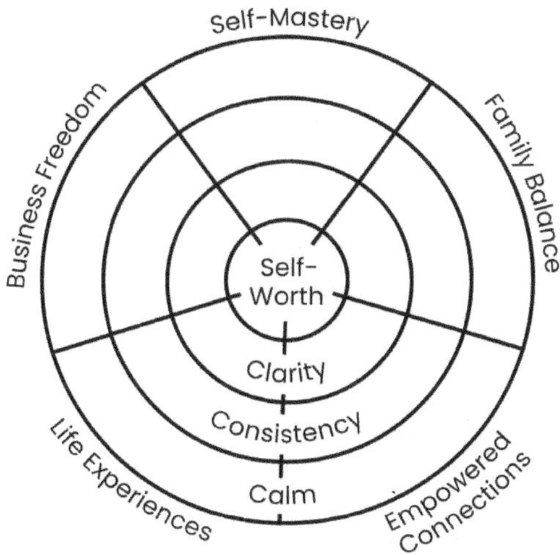

I used to yo-yo diet, obsessed with looking good. For years, I chased the goal of having a six-pack. I went to the gym, tracked progress, and pushed hard, but I was constantly frustrated—never feeling good enough, falling off the wagon, and starting again.

Here's how the S3C Method reframed my health journey:

- *Self-Worth* – I realised my approach to fitness came from fear, not love. I had been told I was "destined to be fat" because I had my mum's genes, and I carried that fear. Healing my self-worth meant shifting to a place of appreciation. Fitness became about loving myself, not punishing myself.

- ***Clarity*** – My goal was wrong. A six-pack for what? For likes on Instagram? I redefined success: to feel energised, to enjoy healthy food without restriction, and to make fitness a fun and sustainable part of life.
- ***Consistency*** – Instead of extreme diets, I focussed on small, steady actions: keeping a food journal, eating in moderation, and staying active daily.
- ***Calm*** – With this perspective shift, I stopped stressing about perfection. I trusted the process, set intentions each morning, and planned my meals and workouts. I even used ChatGPT as my fitness coach to keep me focussed and accountable.

The result? No more yo-yo dieting. Just sustainable health rooted in peace and purpose.

FINAL THOUGHTS

The S3C Method isn't just a catchy acronym, it's a system that works. Turning your life from chaos to clarity. From stress to calm. From empty to fulfilled.

These four steps have transformed my life, my business, and my relationships. They've helped me become the kind of woman, mother, wife, and leader I'm proud to be. And now, it's your turn. We're going to dive deeper into each one; starting with the foundation of it all: Self-Worth and I will be sharing more examples along the way.

REFLECTION QUESTIONS

1. What are some areas you're wrestling with in life right now?
2. If your life was fully aligned with your deepest values, what would change?
3. What patterns, habits, or beliefs have sabotaged your happiness or success in the past?

CHAPTER 7.2

Self-Worth: The Foundation of Fulfilment

"Until you make the unconscious conscious, it will direct your life and you will call it fate." - Carl Jung

If you take only one thing from this entire framework, let it be this: Self-worth is the foundation of everything. Without it, the rest; clarity, consistency, and calm can easily crumble.

You might map out your ideal life.
You might build beautiful habits.
You might even experience moments of peace.

But if you haven't healed the way you see yourself, you'll slip back into old patterns the moment life gets uncomfortable. Why? Because your subconscious programming always runs the show.

The truth about transformation is that we don't get stuck because we're unmotivated. We get stuck because something deeper is pulling us back to what feels familiar, even when it's dysfunctional.

Our brain is wired for safety, not success. And many of our protective patterns were formed long before we knew how to question them. Dr. Nicole LePera, author of *How to Do the Work*, explains that many of our behaviours are shaped by emotional wounds from childhood. These wounds form your core beliefs, things like:

"I'm only lovable if I achieve something."
"I have to prove my worth to be accepted."
"If I stop, I'll fall behind."

THE DISGUISES OF LOW SELF-WORTH

Sometimes, low self-worth doesn't look like insecurity. It looks like ambition. It looks like hustle. It looks like working overtime, saying yes to everything, carrying the weight of the world on your shoulders and calling it *sacrifice*.

One of the most common disguises for low self-worth is overworking in the name of love, telling ourselves we're doing it for the family.

We say things like:

"I'm building this business to give them a better life."

"I just want my kids to have what I never had."

"It's for my partner, so we can finally relax one day."

And while those intentions may be genuine, if we're honest, there's often something deeper underneath. A belief that our worth is tied to how much we do. A fear that slowing down means failing.

A voice whispering, *"You're only valuable when you're useful."*

I've seen it, and believed it. My husband was working non-stop and justifying it with love: *"I'm doing this for the family."* But years would go by and despite his business growth, he was still the same. Same hustle and not present with the family. What my family actually needed was his presence and his time. Not just the money.

Sometimes the most "successful" life on the outside is masking the most disconnected one on the inside.

When your self-worth is unhealed, working harder feels safer than slowing down. Because if you stop... you might have to face the discomfort underneath. The silence. The doubt.

The fear that you're not enough unless you're producing, proving, or providing.

But here's the truth: *Your worth is not measured by your output.* Your family doesn't need your hustle, they need your heart. And ironically, when you lead from healed self-worth, you often become more productive, not less.

You make clearer decisions. You set stronger boundaries. You model what wholeness looks like.

So ask yourself honestly:

Is your hard work rooted in love... or in fear?
Are you truly building for your family or trying to prove your worth through them?
Are you feeling less worthy seeing someone else richer than you?

Even the most high-achieving people carry these hidden scripts. And unless you address them, no level of success will ever feel like enough. Psychologist Abraham Maslow named *'esteem'* as one of the core human needs right after *'safety and belonging'.*

Without it, we seek external validation to regulate our internal state.

Dr. Gabor Maté explains that many high-functioning adults chase productivity and success as a coping mechanism.

We become addicted to doing, not because we love it, but because our nervous system equates stillness with danger.

MY JOURNEY TO RECLAIMING SELF-WORTH

For years, I thought success meant proving myself.

I chased revenue, recognition, and results believing that if I just worked harder and achieved more, I'd finally feel "enough." Deep down, I believed I wasn't worthy of love until I became rich.

That belief was planted early. I remember being about five years old in Vietnam. I asked my dad if I could have some Sprite, the fizzy lemonade soft drink.

He told me it was reserved for guests visiting from overseas. Confused, I asked, *"But why can't I have some?"* He snapped: *"Who do you think you are!?!"*

At that moment, I felt small. Unworthy. Like I wasn't even good enough for a soft drink.

If my dad thought guests were more worthy than his own daughter, I figured I had to become somebody to deserve more. So I made a silent vow: *"I'll show him. One day, I'll be successful enough to deserve the best."*

That wasn't the only moment. Throughout my childhood, my parents made remarks like *"You're dumb,"* or *"You'll never be rich, it's just not your destiny."* I internalised it all. I carried that weight into adulthood. Yes, it made me driven. But it also made me bitter.

Years later, during a powerful coaching session with Uma, I finally saw the root. I was succeeding; not from love, but from resentment. Not to fulfil my potential, but to prove my parents wrong. Uma gave me an exercise I'll never forget:

Write a forgiveness letter. Not to send, but to release.

I wrote a letter thanking my parents for loving me even if they didn't know how to show it. I told them I understood, and I forgave them.

I never gave them the letter. Writing it down was enough to make me cry uncontrollably and release the pain I've felt for years. A massive weight lifted from my shoulders. And in that moment, I realised: I never needed their validation. I never did.

Everything changed. I stopped building my business from bitterness. I started building it from joy. I no longer wanted to prove anything.

I simply wanted to share my success with them.

And now? My relationship with my parents has healed. I've taken them on holidays. I've bought them both cars. But the real transformation happened within. I now believe in my worth not because of fear but because of love.

OVERCOMING SELF-WORTH LIMITATIONS

If we want to live a 360° successful life, we must free ourselves from the need to prove our value. No amount of money, hustle, or recognition will make us feel "enough" if we're still carrying unresolved pain. Until we do the inner work, we'll keep chasing more and still feel empty. Until you believe you're enough, you'll keep trying to prove it. You'll attach your worth to performance, income, appearance, or relationships, none of which will fill the void.

You may build a life that looks great on the outside... But inside, you'll still feel like you're chasing something. You don't need to do more. You need to believe more; in your *intrinsic* worth, before the achievements, before the titles, before the approval. As Michael A. Singer writes in The Untethered Soul:

"You don't have to get rid of fear. You just have to stop believing the voice that tells you you're not enough."

So the question is how do I overcome my self-worth limitations? I highly recommend working with a therapist or life coach like I did. It's the most effective way to uncover and reprogram the subconscious. Tools like 5D Breathwork have also been transformational for me, helping me access my subconscious and release hidden pain. In the meantime, here's a self-reflection exercise to get started:

Step 1: Firstly review the list and circle which limiting beliefs resonate with you the most.

Common Self-Limiting Beliefs Entrepreneurs Struggle With

1. Worthiness & Identity
    - I'm not good enough.
    - If I'm successful, others will get jealous and dislike me
    - I'll never be as good as others.
    - I need to prove others wrong.
    - I'm only valuable if I'm busy or productive.
    - I'm selfish if I put myself first.

2. Fear of Rejection & Belonging

- I have to be perfect to be loved or accepted.
- I have to please others to have value.
- If I say no, people will stop liking me.
- I'll be judged if I speak up.
- I'm "too much" for people.
- My opinion is not as important as others.

3. Comparison & Imposter Syndrome

- I'm an introvert and shy.
- There's no point starting because others are already doing it better.
- I'll never catch up, I'm already too far behind.
- I don't have enough experience or credentials to be taken seriously.
- I'm not lucky like others.
- They're a natural at that (skill), I'm not.

4. Perfectionism & Fear of Failure

- I'm a failure because I've failed before.
- If I don't put myself out there, then I can't fail.
- If I make a mistake, people will lose respect for me.
- I will lose face, if things don't go my way.
- I have to have all the answers before I can start.
- I'm not going to do something, unless I can do it perfectly

5. Age, Background & Circumstances

- I'm too old/too young to make a change.
- It's too late for me to start over.
- I can't do that because I'm a man/woman.
- My circumstances (family, culture, location) limits me
- I don't want to disappoint my parents
- I have to wait for the "right time" before I can act.

6. Leadership & Capability

- I'm not smart enough to achieve my goals.
- I'm not capable of leading others.
- I'm not creative enough.
- I'm not disciplined enough to succeed.
- I'm not brave enough to take risks.

7. Money & Success

- I'm not good with money.
- I don't like numbers.
- If I don't work hard, I can't make money
- I'm selfish if I put myself first.
- If I charge more, I will look greedy
- I can't succeed and still be a good parent/partner.

8. Rest, Time & Control

- Rest is lazy. If I'm not grinding, I'm falling behind.
- If I slow down, I'll lose everything I've built.
- If I delegate, things won't be done properly.
- It's faster if I do just do it
- I can never catch up
- Opportunities only come once, if I miss them, I'm done.

9. Asking for Help & Vulnerability

- Asking for help means I'm weak.
- It's not safe to be vulnerable or show weakness.
- If I shine too brightly, I'll make others uncomfortable.
- Other people's opinions matter more than my own.
- My voice or story isn't worth sharing.

10. Body Image

- I'm not attractive enough.
- I'm too short/tall
- I'll only be lovable when I look a certain way.
- I look old
- I can't feel confident until I reach my "ideal" weight.
- People won't take me seriously because of how I look.

11. Relationships

- I'm bad at relationships and always will be.
- I have to sacrifice my needs to keep others happy.
- Love never lasts for me.
- I'll be abandoned if I show the real me.
- I'm too damaged to have a healthy relationship.
- I'm not worthy of true love.

Step 2: Now I want you to look at the beliefs you circled.

Which three feel like they have the biggest impact on your self-worth right now? Write them below:

1. ______________________________
2. ______________________________
3. ______________________________

Step 3: For each belief, write a new empowering belief that challenges and replaces it. Make it personal, positive, and present tense (as if it's already true).

1. ______________________________
2. ______________________________
3. ______________________________

Examples:

1. Limiting Belief: I'm bad at relationships and always will be.

-> Empowering Belief: *"My past relationships have given me wisdom and helped me grow. I am becoming a better partner every day. The right person for me will come, and together we will create a loving, supportive relationship."*

2. Limiting Belief: I can't feel confident until I reach my "ideal" weight.

-> Empowering Belief: *"How I look does not define me. I am grateful for my health, my energy, and the gift of being alive. I nourish my body with healthy food and move it in ways that feel good. I embrace my body as it is today and celebrate the journey I'm on."*

3. Limiting Belief: If I slow down, I'll lose everything I've built.

-> Empowering Belief: *"Rest makes me stronger and gives me the clarity to grow sustainably. Life is not just about the destination — it's about enjoying the journey. I choose to be present, savour the moment, and trust that everything will always work out for my good."*

Once you've recreated your new empowering beliefs, commit to them for 30 days. Sit with them every morning when you wake up and every night before you go to bed. Don't just repeat the words, feel them as if they are already true.

A hack I use, is to think about my children. How would they feel if I lived out these new beliefs? Would I want them to inherit my old limiting ones or see me embody new, life-giving truths? When I picture myself modelling these beliefs for my kids, it gives me a deeper motivation to change. It reminds me that transformation isn't just about me, it's about the legacy I leave for them.

FINAL THOUGHTS

This journey isn't about becoming someone new. It's about returning to the version of you who already knew you were enough, before the world taught you to doubt it.

There's a reason the S3C Method begins with Self-Worth.

Because you can have the clearest goals (Clarity), the strongest habits (Consistency), and even the calmest moments (Calm)...

But if your worth is still tied to achievement or approval, you'll keep sabotaging your growth when life gets hard.

This isn't just personal development, it's identity work. And when your identity is rooted in unshakable self-worth, you stop needing external proof to feel valuable.

In the next chapter, we will delve into the next important pillar of the S3C method; Clarity.

ACTION STEPS

1. **Spot Your Pattern:** When you feel "not enough," what do you do; overwork, numb out, seek validation? Awareness is the first step to freedom.
2. **Inner Child Reconnection:** Picture your younger self. What did they long to hear? Write those words down and speak them over yourself today.
3. **Forgiveness Letter:** Who do you need to forgive? Write a letter to them and permit yourself to move on from past pains.

CHAPTER 7.3

Clarity: Define Your Vision, Direct Your Life

"People are not lazy. They simply have impotent goals—that is, goals that do not inspire them." - Tony Robbins

Clarity is the key to momentum. This chapter is the second step in Linh's Life System; the S3C Method. In the previous chapter, we explored the foundation of fulfilment: Self-Worth. Once you believe you're worthy of more, you need to know what that "more" actually looks like and that's where clarity comes in. We already explored key clarity foundations in

Section 2 where you defined your vision, aligned with your values, and clarified goals that matter.

This chapter builds on that foundation and helps you activate it in your daily life so that your identity, direction, and decisions all align with the life you're here to create.

WHEN I THOUGHT I WAS CLEAR (BUT WASN'T)

For a long time, I thought I was clear.

I had goals.
I had vision boards.
I had a business plan.

But when I looked deeper... I realised I was still chasing success on someone else's terms. I was ticking off boxes without ever asking, *Are these even the right boxes for me?* It wasn't until I paused and truly reflected that I saw how much of my energy was going toward things that didn't align with my core values. I said yes too often. I filled my calendar, but felt empty. I was productive, but not fulfilled. Clarity changed everything.

I started asking deeper questions:

1. What does success mean to me; as a mum, a wife, a leader, a friend, a daughter?
2. What does a great day or year actually look like?
3. Who am I trying to become, not just what am I trying to achieve?

You can't lead your life or your business without knowing where you're going and why it matters.

Most people aren't unmotivated.

They're simply moving fast in the wrong direction.

They're chasing goals based on what others expect. They're ticking off to-do lists but drifting from purpose. They're growing but not grounded.

That's why so many high achievers feel lost, even after they've "made it." They've climbed the ladder only to realise it's leaning against the wrong wall.

When you lack clarity, everything feels heavy. You might know the feeling:

- *You say family is your top priority, but your calendar tells a different story*
- *You're chasing goals, but can't remember why anymore*
- *You're accomplishing more than ever but feeling more drained than ever*

This isn't a time management problem, it's a clarity gap. When your vision is vague, your life becomes reactive. But when your vision is clear and values-aligned, your energy becomes focused and powerful.

But your vision isn't a one-size-fits-all. We live in a noisy world, flooded with content, courses, and advice on what success should look like. But clarity doesn't come from comparison.

It comes from within. You must define success on your own terms. Otherwise, you'll spend your life chasing goals that never bring you fulfilment.

Simon Sinek puts it perfectly:

> *"Working hard for something we don't care about is called stress. Working hard for something we love is called passion."*

REDEFINING SUCCESS FOR ME

I used to believe success meant constant growth, more clients, more revenue, more milestones. But I realised I was chasing a version of success that didn't feel true to me. Through journalling, coaching, and slowing down, I redefined success to include being fully present with my family, running a business that supports my life rather than consumes it, and prioritising health, faith, and peace not just profit.

I began creating white space in my calendar to breathe, think, and simply be. Most importantly, I started setting goals that were measurable and crystal clear because vague aspirations weren't enough anymore.

I defined what happiness looked like in my everyday life. That meant planning two holidays a year to disconnect and recharge, locking in monthly date nights with my husband to nurture our relationship, and intentionally increasing the frequency of small joys that make life richer: *whether it's time with friends, hobbies I love, or moments of stillness.* Then I revisit that definition regularly because what success looks like evolves with each season of life.

THE 3 LAYERS OF CLARITY

In my experience, clarity has three powerful layers. When all three align, you move with purpose, peace, and power.

1. Clarity of Identity: Who are you at your core?

This is about knowing who you are when no one's watching and making decisions from that truth. Ask:

- What do I deeply value?
- What kind of energy do I want to bring into the world?
- What makes me feel most alive and most me?

2. Clarity of Vision: What are you building, and why?

This is your personal blueprint for the life and legacy you want to create. Ask:

- What kind of life, business, family, and future do I want?
- What does "success" actually look like for me?

3. Clarity of Action: How does this show up day to day?

This is where real alignment happens or doesn't. Ask:

- Do my habits, routines, and boundaries reflect my values and vision?
- Am I living in alignment or just performing?

When your identity, vision, and daily actions are in sync, life becomes lighter. You stop second-guessing, stop chasing everything and move forward with confidence, clarity, and calm.

RELATIONSHIP PRIORITIES: ROLES CLARITY EXERCISE

One of the biggest sources of overwhelm comes from the many roles we juggle in life.

We're entrepreneurs, parents, partners, friends, leaders, and community members, sometimes all in the same day.

When we don't consciously define how we want to show up in each role, we end up reacting to whatever life throws at us. That's when we feel scattered, drained, or like we're failing everywhere.

This exercise is designed to help you step back, look at the key roles you play, and bring clarity to them. When you define *who you want to be* and *what you want to do* in each role, you stop operating on autopilot and start living with intention.

Instead of *wishing* you could be more present with your kids, get specific. What does "being present" actually look like for you? Is it putting your phone away at the dinner table? Scheduling a weekly one-on-one outing with each child? Reading together for 15 minutes before bed?

Clarity means creating a clear plan for how and how often you'll show up, so you know exactly what to do to create the feeling you desire. Presence isn't built from good intentions alone, it's built from intentional actions repeated consistently.

Think of this as your personal operating manual. It's not about doing everything perfectly, it's about giving yourself a compass for how you want to show up in the moments that matter most.

Step 1: List Your Roles

Write down the main roles you currently play in your life. These could include:

- Partner (wife, husband, girlfriend, boyfriend)
- Parent (mum, dad, step-parent)
- Family (daughter, son, sibling, grandchild)
- Business (entrepreneur, leader, manager, colleague)
- Personal (friend, community member, volunteer, student of life)
- Self (your role to yourself: health, faith, personal growth)

(**Tip:** Don't forget the "self" role. Many of us neglect it, but you can't show up fully for others if you don't show up for yourself.)

Step 2: Define "Who I Want to Be"

For each role, ask: What qualities, values, and energy do I want to bring into this role?

Examples:

- As a mum: patient, fun, nurturing.
- As a leader: clear, empowering, fair.
- As a friend: supportive, reliable, encouraging.

Step 3: Define "What I Want to Do"

Now, turn those qualities into actions, habits, and commitments.

Examples:

- As a mum: plan a weekly one-on-one activity with each child, put the phone down during family dinner.
- As a leader: schedule regular check-ins, celebrate team wins, give feedback constructively.
- As a friend: call or message once a month, remember birthdays, organise coffee catch-ups.

Step 4: Reflect

Look at your answers and ask:

- Which role is thriving right now?
- Which role needs more of my attention or intention?
- Where am I showing up out of alignment with the person I want to be?

Example Worksheet Table

Role	**Who I Want to Be** (Qualities & Values)	**What I Want to Do** (Actions & Commitments)
Wife	Loving, supportive, fun	Plan monthly date nights, show appreciation daily
Leader	Inspiring, clear, empowering	Hold regular check-ins, celebrate wins, give constructive feedback
Friend	Present, encouraging, trustworthy	Check in monthly, remember special dates, plan catch-ups

Tip: Don't try to do everything at once. Choose one role where small shifts could make the biggest difference right now, and start there.

FINAL THOUGHTS

We laid the foundation for clarity in Section 2, and now through the S3C Method, you've taken the second step toward a fully aligned life. Clarity is not a luxury, it's a necessity. Without it, your energy gets scattered. Your calendar gets full. And your fulfilment gets postponed. But when you get clear:

- You stop reacting and start creating
- You stop striving blindly and start living intentionally
- You stop saying yes to everything and start saying yes to what truly matters

Clarity won't guarantee you'll never feel lost again. But it will give you the compass to find your way back, every single time.

ACTION STEPS

1. **Define Success for This Season:**
   Ask yourself: "What does success look and feel like for me right now?"
2. **Clarify Who You're Becoming:**
   Write down 3 identity-based statements: "I am someone who... [e.g. protects my energy, leads with heart, prioritises family]."
3. **Audit Your Calendar:**
   Review last week. Highlight what felt aligned, and what didn't. Adjust your upcoming week accordingly.

CHAPTER 7.4

Consistency: Create Rhythms That Support The Life You Want

In the earlier chapters, we explored how to design your life with intention and master your time and energy. But even the most beautifully planned life can crumble if we don't follow through.

That's where consistency comes in, the often-overlooked superpower that turns clarity into progress and vision into results. Consistency is the heartbeat of the S3C Method. It's the difference between starting and becoming. Between dipping your toe in and diving fully into the life you say you want.

As entrepreneurs, we all want to improve ourselves. We want more success in all areas of our life. And in those moments, we often look for one big breakthrough to solve everything. But real transformation doesn't come from a single lightning bolt of motivation.

It comes from the small, often boring actions you do daily, especially when no one's watching.

> *"There is no such thing as time management. There is only self-management."* — Rory Vaden

That quote shook me. I spent years believing my problem was time; not enough hours, too many commitments. But the truth was, I didn't have a time problem. I had a self-leadership problem. I was letting life happen to me, instead of living by design. Eventually, I realised: Your results are not built on what you do occasionally when you feel inspired. They're built on what you do consistently, regardless of how you feel.

And consistency isn't about perfection. It's about trust. Every time I chose to show up; whether to journal, exercise or simply wake up early, I cast a vote for the person I wanted to become.

THE SHIFT THAT CHANGES EVERYTHING: IDENTITY

Before you can show up consistently, you have to believe you're the kind of person who does. You can write goals, create vision boards, and download all the habit-tracking apps. But if your identity is still rooted in who you used to be, not who you're *becoming,* then you'll always self-sabotage. Why? Because deep down, we don't act according to what we want, we act according to who we *believe* we are.

That's why the most powerful shift you can make isn't about your schedule, it's about your self-concept.

I used to think waking up at 3 a.m. was only for extreme CEOs or famous celebrities. But then I met someone who actually did it, a person in real life. Suddenly, I believed it was possible for me too. The thought went from, *"That's impossible for me"* to *"If she can do it, so can I."*

Something similar happened with my mum.

She'd struggled with her weight her entire life. Then she visited Bali and met one of my team members who had transformed her body through intermittent fasting, and in that moment, something clicked. She believed it could be done. She came home, committed, and seven years later, she's still living that new version of herself. She went from a size 14 to a size 8. She didn't just become someone who lost weight, she became an inspiration to her friends in their 60s, showing them that no matter your age or background, you can change if you truly want to. In short, you can't change your life until you change the story you tell yourself.

I AM, I CAN, I GET TO: A POWERFUL MINDSET HACK

As mentioned, the biggest struggle with consistency isn't that we don't know what to do, it's the internal dialogue that makes us doubt whether we can keep doing it.

That's why I use this simple mindset reset whenever I feel resistance creeping in:

" I am. I can. I get to."

It may seem simple, but this three-part inner script has helped me stay consistent even when motivation fades.

Because the truth is, consistency doesn't come from force. It comes from alignment with who you believe you are, what you believe you're capable of, and how you view the process.

1. "I am."

When you're struggling to achieve a goal, or habit. Firstly, catch what you're saying about yourself. Then turn that negative identity into something empowering.

What you believe about yourself becomes the foundation of your habits. If you constantly say, *"I'm a procrastinator"* or *"I'm a starter and not a finisher,"* you're reinforcing an identity that makes it hard to follow through.

But when you shift your self-talk to something like, *"I am someone who follows through, even when it's hard,"* or "*I am becoming a person who honours their word,"* you give yourself permission to act from a different place, a more empowered identity. You don't have to be perfect to start. But you do have to believe that change is possible.

2. "I can."

This is where capability comes in. If you're trying to build a habit but deep down you don't believe you can do it, you'll find every excuse to quit or subconsciously sabotage yourself.

Sometimes the easiest way to build belief is to look for proof even if it's someone else's story. Who do you know that has done what you want to do? It makes your brain say, *"Well, if they can do it, maybe I can too."*

And from there, all you need to do is break it down into the next simple step. You don't need to have it all figured out.

Just enough to move forward. Because confidence doesn't magically appear, it grows through action.

3. "I get to."

This part changes the energy behind everything. When we see habits as chores or punishments e.g. *"I have to eat healthy, I have to wake up early, I have to stop scrolling"*, it creates resistance. But when you reframe it as a privilege, everything softens.

You start to think, *"I get to nourish my body with good food. I get to move because I'm blessed with a working body. I get to show up for my goals because not everyone gets the same chance."*

This mindset doesn't just keep you going, it helps you enjoy the process. You're no longer dragging yourself toward your goals. You're walking with purpose, fuelled by gratitude.

So the next time you feel yourself slipping, say it to yourself: "I am becoming the kind of person who stays consistent. If (that person) can do it, so can I. I get to build this life, one habit at a time."

WHY MOST GOALS FAIL (AND WHAT TO DO INSTEAD)

Let's be real: we don't fail because we don't know what to do. We fail because we don't stay connected to why it matters. A lot of people set goals that sound good on paper; lose weight, make more money, hit a new revenue target, but they're often chasing extrinsic goals.

They subconsciously set goals based on what others expect, what they think will make them feel "enough," or what society celebrates.

But the goals that actually stick, the ones that create real, lasting change are intrinsic. They come from a place of purpose, alignment, and identity.

They're about becoming who you were always meant to be, not proving something to the world. Here's the goal-setting framework I use to ground my habits in real meaning. I don't skim through this list, I go deep.

The more intentional prep work you do before setting a goal, the more likely you are to stick with it.

1. What is your goal?
2. Why is it deeply important to you?
3. How will you feel when you achieve it?
4. What specific actions will you take?
5. What could sabotage your progress?
6. How can you minimise the chances of that happening?
7. What empowering beliefs will you choose to fuel you forward?

Don't rush this part. These questions are the foundation that will carry you through the days when motivation disappears.

THE HABIT SYSTEM THAT ACTUALLY WORKS

Why most people fail and how to do it differently. Most people don't lack goals. They lack systems. That's one of the most powerful truths I took from Atomic Habits book by James Clear, where he writes:

"You don't rise to the level of your goals. You fall to the level of your systems."

In the book, James outlines four laws of behaviour change to help you build better habits and break bad ones:

1. **Make it Obvious:** Use cues in your environment to trigger the habit. Want to drink more water? Keep a full bottle on your desk where you can see it.
2. **Make it Attractive:** Pair the habit with something enjoyable.
3. **Make it Easy:** Reduce friction. Start with small, manageable steps that feel effortless.
4. **Make it Satisfying:** Add a reward so your brain wants to repeat the habit.

These rules are simple but powerful. They help shift the focus away from willpower (which fades) and toward intentional design (which lasts). But as someone juggling business, motherhood, marriage, and self-care, I needed a version that felt even more practical. Something that worked in the real world, across all areas of life, not just in theory. That's how I created Linh's Habits Rules:

MAKE IT EASY. MAKE IT OBVIOUS. MAKE IT LEVERAGED. MAKE IT DAILY.

Let me break it down with an example, say you're trying to build a consistent habit around improving your health:

1. Make it Easy

Remove the resistance and build options into your life. I like to keep multiple forms of exercise ready; walks, treadmill, gym sessions, PT, Pilates, even VR fitness games. That way, there's always something that works, whether I'm short on time, stuck indoors, or lacking energy. Aim for 30 minutes, not an hour. I tell myself: "Just 30 minutes of active time today." That's enough to keep momentum without feeling overwhelming.

2. Make it Obvious

Design your environment so the next step is clear and visible. Wake up and put your gym clothes on straight away. Place your alarm outside your bedroom so you have to get out of bed to turn it off.

Let your surroundings guide you into action without relying on motivation.

3. Make it Leveraged

Entrepreneurs love feeling productive and efficient so use that to your advantage. Stack your habit with something that fuels another area of life. Go for a walk while making a business or personal call (Connection), or listen to an inspiring podcast while working out (Self-Mastery). You'll feel like you're winning twice.

4. Make it Daily

Daily habits create identity. And when something becomes part of your daily rhythm, you stop negotiating with yourself. If you aim to be active 7 days a week, you'll likely hit 5 or 6. But if you aim for 3, you'll procrastinate until the last two days and often only manage one (if any). Daily removes the mental drama. It builds momentum, not guilt. Make good habits be part of your daily routine

These 4 steps are my take on James Clear's method, it has helped me to stick to my habits of staying healthy or waking up early everyday. Try it out for yourself.

THE SPEED TRAP

Why slowing down is the secret to lasting change. One of the biggest mindset shifts I've had to make and now teach often is letting go of the obsession with speed. We live in a world that celebrates quick wins, overnight success, and hustle culture. But in real life, fast often fails. What we need isn't more intensity, it's more sustainability.

I call this pressure to "hurry up and succeed" = the speed trap. It's when we focus so hard on getting there fast that we forget to build a foundation that can actually support us once we arrive. It shows up in different ways:

- Trying to overhaul your whole life in a week
- Expecting instant results from a new habit
- Pushing yourself hard with no room for rest
- Quitting when progress feels slow
- Believing you've failed if you're not perfect

I used to do this all the time, especially when it came to health. I can't tell you how many crash diets and fitness challenges I've done, only to fall back into old habits the moment the challenge ended. I'd go hard, lose some weight, then slowly gain it back... again and again. And it's not just me. We see it even in the most successful people.

- Arianna Huffington collapsed from exhaustion and burnout, hitting her head on her desk and waking up in a pool of blood. That experience forced her to rethink how she defined success and she went on to found Thrive Global to help others avoid the same trap.
- Elon Musk, though celebrated for his brilliance, has openly admitted to sleeping on the Tesla factory floor, working 120-hour weeks, and suffering breakdowns due to chronic overwork. He has even said it's not sustainable and not recommended.

You don't need to do everything at once. You just need to do the right things often.

Everyday Truths That Break the Speed Trap:

- You don't get white teeth by brushing for 30 minutes a day for a month and then stopping. You brush for 2–3 minutes every day. Forever.
- You don't build a great marriage by taking your partner on one lavish holiday a year. It's the small, daily moments; your tone, your attention, your appreciation that keep love alive.

- You don't build a thriving business from one viral launch. It's built from the daily effort: following up, improving systems, showing up for your team and customers consistently.

The Difference Between Fast & Furious vs Slow & Steady

Fast & Furious leads to:	**Slow & Steady leads to:**
Burnout	Long-term growth
Guilt	Habits that stick
All-or-nothing mindset	Identity-level change
Quitting when it gets hard	A lifestyle you can actually maintain

I used to think if I wasn't doing it "perfectly" or fast enough, I was failing. But now I realise: success isn't about speed. It's about staying power. Don't aim to arrive. Aim to become.

Instead of asking, How fast can I get there? Ask:

1. *Who do I need to become to live this way consistently?*
2. *How can I design habits I can sustain, not just survive?*

Whether it's health, marriage, business, real transformation doesn't come from going harder. It comes from going longer.

Let go of the rush. Build the life you want by becoming the person who lives it daily.

THE ONE THING

There's a question I came across in the book The One Thing by Gary Keller that changed everything for me:

> *"What's the one thing I can do such that by doing it, everything else becomes easier or unnecessary?"*

At first, it sounded like just another productivity idea, but the simplicity of it stuck with me. I kept thinking about it. So I asked myself honestly:

> *"What is the one habit that, if I truly committed to, would make everything else in my life easier?"*

The answer was clear: waking up early. We all know what the "good habits" are: journalling, meditating, praying, planning your day and moving your body. But the reality is, we don't do them consistently. Why? Because we don't feel like we have time. That's what waking up early gave me: time. Time before the chaos of the day. Time before the emails, the kids, the meetings. Time for me. Waking up early became the one thing that unlocked all the other habits I knew were good for me but kept skipping. I didn't need more motivation, I needed more margin. That one habit created space for:

- Prayer and journalling
- Movement and reflection
- Planning my day with intention
- Peace and quiet before giving to everyone else

I wasn't reacting to my day anymore. I was leading it with calm, clarity, and energy. Years later, I found myself in a different season and asked a new version of the same question:

"What's the one thing I need to remove that would make everything else easier?"

The answer? Alcohol. Even though I wasn't drinking heavily, I noticed the subtle ways it was sabotaging my mornings. A couple of glasses of wine meant disrupted sleep, less motivation, and more resistance to the very habits I knew made me feel good.

I had the intention to have a good day but alcohol was quietly working against it.

ALCOHOL: THE BIGGEST SABOTEUR OF CONSISTENCY

I've spoken about alcohol earlier in this book, but I want to revisit it here, because it deserves that level of attention. If there's one habit that has the power to quietly undo your progress, it's this one.

Let me share a personal story, because for me, alcohol was the biggest saboteur of my consistency. It was the one habit that completely misaligned with who I wanted to be. I saw myself as someone who valued health, who wanted to be a good example to others. But drinking made me someone I didn't recognise, someone who said unkind things to my husband, who was too hungover to drive the kids to school, too tired to work out, and too foggy to lead my team.

Every time I drank, I felt guilt and shame. And yet, I couldn't stop. I told myself things like:

"I can't have fun without alcohol"

"What will I do if I don't drink?"

"Wouldn't life be boring?"

I'd been drinking since I was 16. I was known as the party girl, and alcohol was woven into my identity. I drank to escape, to socialise, to celebrate. Like many entrepreneurs, I thought drinking was normal, even expected, at events, dinners, and parties. As much as I hated how it robbed me of mental clarity and made me inconsistent in all the areas that mattered most, I couldn't break free. I tried everything from moderation rules, dry months, even an eight-month alcohol-free streak. But nothing stuck.

Until 2 April 2023.

After losing two phones in the span of two months due to alcohol-related incidents, I reached my breaking point. Enough was enough. I decided to quit, for good. But this time was different. Two months before that decision, I had found a new church Potters House in Fairfield.

I quickly noticed that most people there didn't drink. And yet they were fun, kind, full of joy. They showed me that life could be full without alcohol. My belief shifted once again...*"If they can do it, so can I."* What inspired me most was that they didn't just quit for themselves, they quit to help others. That hit me deeply. I thought, Wow... now that's purpose-driven.

My why shifted from *"I want to be better"* to *"I want to be a role model for others, too."* When I decided to quit, I also decided to change my environment. I intentionally avoided people and places that made it easy to fall back into old habits. I stopped going to social settings where drinking was the norm and instead surrounded myself with people who lived alcohol-free. Over time, I grew strong enough to be in those environments again, without temptation. Here's what helped me stay on track:

- I joined the I Am Sober app to connect with others on the same journey
- I stocked up on non-alcoholic alternatives at home
- I unfollowed triggering accounts and filled my feed with sober inspiration
- I reminded myself of my why every time temptation crept in

Eventually, it got easier. Now, 3 years later, I can confidently say: I'm the happiest I've ever been.

- I no longer wake up with sluggish, regret-filled mornings
- I show up sharper, more energised, and more consistent
- I've saved time, energy, and thousands of dollars
- And I've inspired others to question their own relationship with alcohol

Overall quitting was hard. But the freedom, clarity, and confidence I've gained? Absolutely worth it. So if you're an entrepreneur who drinks to "unwind" or "connect," ask yourself honestly: Is it actually helping you or is it quietly costing you more than you realise?

WHY YOU MIGHT FALL OFF TRACK (AND HOW TO GET BACK ON)

There will be times when you fall off track. Even with the best intentions, consistency can slip through your fingers.

Falling off a habit doesn't necessarily mean you're lazy or lacking discipline, it usually means something in your environment, mindset, or systems is out of sync.

Here's a checklist to help you pinpoint why things may have derailed and how to realign quickly and effectively.

1. Your Identity Doesn't Match the Habit: You're trying to behave like someone you haven't fully become in your mind.

How to get back on: Start using identity-based language: "I'm someone who..." Track your wins. Visualise your future self and let that guide your decisions.

2. Your Motivation Is Extrinsic: You're doing it for validation, not values.

How to get back on: Ask, "If no one saw this, would I still want it?" Reconnect to values like peace, alignment, freedom.

3. Your 'Why' Isn't Deep Enough: The habit feels shallow or disconnected from emotion.

How to get back on: Ask: "Who else benefits when I follow through?" Make it personal, emotional, legacy-driven.

4. Your Environment Doesn't Support You: Your setup pulls you back into old patterns.

How to get back on: Remove triggers, design visual cues, spend time with aligned people.

5. Your Systems Are Missing or Inflexible: You're relying on memory or willpower.

How to get back on: Build structure. Use a habit tracker, calendar, and alarms. Set yourself up for success.

6. You're Lacking Accountability or Support: You're going it alone.

How to get back on: Get a buddy, coach, or VA. Join a supportive community. Make your goals visible.

7. You're Expecting Perfection Instead of Progress: One mistake leads to quitting.

How to get back on: Redefine success. Say, "I will return quickly." Track progress, not perfection.

Remember consistency isn't about never slipping.

It's about learning how to get back on track faster each time. The more you show up, the more you start to trust yourself. That trust spills into every part of your life, your marriage, your health, your parenting, your business. You become someone who doesn't just talk about change.

You become someone who lives it. On the flip side, every time you break a promise to yourself, your belief takes a hit. That's why I always say: don't aim for perfection, aim for progress. Win today. Then win again tomorrow. Let those wins compound.

FINAL THOUGHTS

Consistency isn't about being perfect, it's about showing up with purpose, even on the days you don't feel like it. It's not just a habit you build, it's a relationship you form with yourself.

When your habits align with who you're becoming, and your systems support the life you want to live, consistency stops feeling like discipline and starts feeling like freedom. Because the truth is, you don't need more motivation. You need clearer identity, stronger systems, and a deeper *why.*

Small, meaningful actions done over and over are what create a life of peace, power, and purpose.

So start small. Stay aligned. And keep returning, because the person you want to be is built one rhythm at a time.

REFLECTION PROMPTS

1. What's one habit that if I mastered it, it would make everything else easier?
2. What system or environment change could make this habit easier?
3. Am I chasing this goal for someone else's approval or my own alignment?

CHAPTER 7.5

Calm: The Fuel That Keeps You Grounded

You can have clarity. You can be consistent. But if you're not calm, you won't feel any of it. Calm isn't a bonus. It's a requirement. It's what steadies your spirit so you can keep going, not in a frantic sprint, but in a grounded rhythm.

This chapter explores the third "C" in my S3C Method, the happiness system I created to help entrepreneurs move from burnout to balance. Clarity gives you direction. Consistency gives you momentum. But Calm? Calm gives you fuel. Without it, everything else eventually falls apart.

In my experience, most entrepreneurs *know* what to do. They've set the goals, made the plans, and committed to new routines. But then, life happens. Stress creeps in. And slowly, everything starts to unravel. That's not a failure of discipline. It's usually a lack of calming techniques and the ability to self-soothe that sends those intentions flying out the window.

CALM IS AN INTERNAL STRATEGY

We often think of calm as something external, *"I'll feel calm once this project is done"* or *"once the kids are back at school."* But calm is an internal practice. It's about how you hold space for yourself in a noisy world.

> *"Set peace of mind as your highest goal and organise your life around it."* — Brian Tracy

In the workshop I held for a group of entrepreneurs who are my fellow EO members, I talked about the difference between creating space and just filling space.

So many high-achievers wake up early only to rush into replying to emails and check their social media. One of my friends proudly told me she finally started waking up early... To do the dishes. I laughed and gently said, "You've just traded one form of unproductive busyness for another."

Creating space means intentionally carving out moments that nourish your nervous system and restore your spirit. Not every pocket of time needs to be filled with doing.

Sometimes, it's about *being*. It means sitting with your thoughts, setting an intention for the day, reflecting on what went well and what you think needs improvement. Morning is a sacred time, and how you start your day can impact the rest of your day.

GRATITUDE: MY LIFE CHANGING PRACTICE

One of the most powerful practices I've built over the past 15 years is writing down three things I'm grateful for every day. I first learned this from Oprah.

At the time, I was going through so much that I honestly felt I had *nothing* to be grateful for. No boyfriend, no money, no relationship with my parents... I really felt that I didn't have anything.

But I decided to try. If Oprah, Tony Robbins and other successful people suggest to practise gratitude because it worked for them, then why not give it a go.

I remember the first time I was writing my gratitude, it was hard. I would sit there thinking, *"I've got nothing." But as I forced myself to think, I started writing things like:*

1. A warm cup of coffee
2. My affectionate son
3. A warm sunny day

That simple act, writing it down shifted everything.

Something about 'writing' made it real, it helps me process and shift my energy. It's not enough to just think it in your head, you must write it down, it's a different kind of feeling. I feel better immediately. And on the days that I felt more challenged, I write ten things I'm grateful for instead of three.

If you really think about it, there's always someone worse off, things could have been worse and gratitude helps you zoom out and find perspective.

Think of it this way, would you keep gifting your child things if they're ungrateful and don't say thank you to you? You wouldn't. When we are grateful, God or the Universe will give us more things to be grateful for. When we express gratitude, we will be blessed with more.

Gratitude is part of my life and continues to be the source of calm for me daily, that I've taught my kids from the age of five to practise. At first they also struggled. When I asked them before bed time, what are you grateful for today, they defaulted to thinking about things that went wrong in the day for them. But through regular practice they can now express gratitude easily.

Just recently when my son came 47th out of 50 in his long distance running race, instead of being upset he said he was grateful he didn't come last and that being able to compete in this race was already special because not all his classmate made it into this selective race. I was so proud of his perspective and I didn't have to deal with a tantrum throwing kid, the 'bad loser' type.

The way I journal my gratitude now is by using the Gratitude app or Notion. It's digital, so I can access the notes anytime. Writing in a notebook is fine too, it's just harder to re-read it when you want to revisit.

OTHERS PRACTICES THAT ANCHOR YOU

Here are some other calm-building rituals that help me return to stillness:

- **Prayer:** Talking to God reminds me I'm not in control, He is.
- **Walking in nature:** A simple walk can reset your entire nervous system.
- **Breathwork or meditation:** These help me shift from reaction to intention.
- **Taking a bath:** My ultimate recharge moment (with candles and piano relaxing music).
- **Avoiding alcohol:** It may take the edge off in the moment, but often steals clarity and calm the next day.

But Calm is a lifestyle, not just a morning routine, Calm isn't just something you do for 15 minutes in the morning or once a week. It's how you live, lead, and move through the world.

Block out breathing space between meetings, keep your calendar spacious, not stuffed, say "no" to things that cost your peace, let go of control and trust the process

For a long time, I thought calm meant trying to control everything: planning harder, working longer, managing every detail. But control is not calm. In fact, it's often the enemy of it. True calm, I learned, comes from surrender.

It lives in my quiet mornings when I wake before the world, journal my thoughts, breathe deeply, and hand my worries over to God. It lives in the moments I let go of needing to force outcomes and trust that a greater plan is unfolding, even when I can't see it yet.

Calm is an anchor. It doesn't remove the storms, but it steadies you through them. And like any skill, calm can be built. Not overnight.

But with small daily choices; choosing prayer over panic, choosing stillness over scrambling, choosing trust over control.

CALM COMES FROM KNOWING THE PURPOSE BEHIND IT ALL

One of the biggest mindset shifts I've had in my walk with God is this truth: God cares more about your character than your comfort.

That understanding alone has helped me remain calm during storms. I stopped resisting challenges and started embracing them because they're not punishments, they're opportunities.

"Don't wish life were easier, wish you were better."

— Jim Rohn

The hard seasons are where I've grown the most. I don't avoid challenges; I walk through it with faith, knowing it's shaping me into who I'm meant to become. And when things feel unfair or painful, I remind myself of something I learned from Rabbi Daniel Lapin: Your life is like a video, not a photo.

In other words, what seems bad right now may be the very thing that blesses you later. But you won't see it if you freeze the frame and judge too soon. Let the video play. Let your life unfold. Calm comes when you trust the full story, even when you're stuck in a difficult scene.

There's a Chinese parable that captures this beautifully; the story of the old farmer.

One day, the farmer's horse ran away.
His neighbours said, *"What bad luck!"*
The farmer simply replied, *"Maybe yes, maybe no."*

The next day, the horse returned and brought back three wild horses.
The neighbours said, *"How wonderful!"*
The farmer replied again, *"Maybe yes, maybe no."*

The following day, the farmer's son tried to ride one of the wild horses, but fell and broke his leg.
The neighbours cried, *"How terrible!"*
The farmer, steady as ever, said, *"Maybe yes, maybe no."*

A few weeks later, soldiers came to the village to recruit all the young men for war but they left the farmer's son behind because of his broken leg. The farmer's son was spared from having to go to war.

The point is: you never know what a moment really means until you see how the story unfolds. When you live with that mindset when you stop labelling everything as good or bad in the moment you begin to develop true calmness.

A calm that's not based on circumstances, but on trust. A calm rooted in the belief that everything, even the setbacks, is part of something greater.

Let the video play.

God's not finished with the scene you're in.

THE CONTROL TEST: YOUR SHORTCUT TO SANITY

When life feels chaotic, ask yourself: *What's within my control and what's not?*

Draw a line down the middle of a piece of paper. On one side, write what's *within* your control. On the other side, write what's *outside* your control.

For example:

- **Outside My Control:** The economy, interest rates, tax policies, global events, other people's opinions, the past.
- **Within My Control:** My business model, how I manage costs, my sales strategy, how I respond to challenges, my daily habits and mindset, what I choose to focus on.

For example, if a team member misinterprets your message and complains to others, you can't control their reaction but you *can* choose how you respond. That's where peace lives: in the space between what happens and how you handle it. And in business? You can't control the economy or global trends. But you can cut expenses, pivot your offers, or reframe your mindset.

Calm doesn't come from the market, it comes from your personal response to it. This exercise may seem simple, but it's incredibly grounding. It helps you stop spiralling over things you can't change and shift your energy to where it actually makes a difference. Instead of worrying about what you can't control, focus on what you can. When you focus on what you can control, your power comes back and you move from stress into strategy.

Because when your nervous system is calm, everything else works better, your focus sharpens, your leadership deepens, and your joy becomes more sustainable.

CALM REQUIRES TRUTH, NOT JUST TECHNIQUES

One of the reasons calm is so elusive is because we don't respond to *reality*, we respond to our *perception* of reality.

In his book *The Courage to Be You*, Joe Pane outlines something that forever changed the way I interpret stressful situations. He explains that most of our stress comes from not being able to separate fact from fiction. We don't take things at face value. Instead, we add meaning, assumptions, and interpretations and then react to that.

Joe explains there are three types of truth:

1. Imagined Truth

This is what we make up. The stories, worst-case scenarios, and what-ifs that spiral in our heads.

Example: Your client doesn't reply to your proposal. You immediately think, "They must have hated it. I probably messed up. They're never going to work with me again."

Reality? They might just be sick or caught up in other priorities.

2. Assumed Truth

This is what we believe to be true without checking the facts, usually based on past experience or bias.

Example: A team member looks upset in a meeting, and you assume they're unhappy with your leadership. You start to feel anxious or defensive. Later, you find out they had a personal issue that had nothing to do with you.

3. Actual Truth

This is what is verifiably true. It's based on facts and evidence.

Example: The client hasn't responded. That's it. That's the only actual truth right now. Anything beyond that is imagination or assumption.

The magic happens when we pause and ask ourselves:

"What is the actual truth here?"

This simple question has helped me stay calm in high-pressure situations. Because when you realise most of your stress is self-generated and that you have the power to rewrite the story, everything softens.

Your heart rate slows. Your thoughts become clearer. You move from reaction to reflection. This doesn't mean you ignore reality. It means you face it without the noise.

CALM & JOY MENU

Stress will come and that's part of life. But you don't have to wait until you're overwhelmed to take care of yourself. To make it easy for you, I've created a menu of 60 calming and joyful activities you can build into your daily rhythm. The more you practise them regularly, the stronger your "calm muscle" becomes, so when challenges show up, you're already grounded and resilient.

Review the list and circle the ones that resonate most with you. Choose a few to weave into your weekly routine, and add your own at the bottom. Come back to this menu whenever you want to reset, recharge, or simply add more joy to your life.

Mindset Shifts for Calm

1. Pause before reacting – ask yourself: "Will this matter in a week?"
2. Reframe the story – instead of "This is happening to me," think "This is happening for me."
3. Focus on what you can control – let go of the rest.
4. Zoom out – see the bigger picture, this is just one moment in your life.
5. Assume positive intent – people are rarely trying to hurt you on purpose.
6. Ask better questions – "What's the lesson here?" Instead of "Why me?"

Quick Calm Reset

7. Deep breathing (inhale 4 sec, hold 4 sec, exhale 4 sec)
8. Step outside and feel the fresh air
9. Listen to calming instrumental music
10. Stretch your arms, neck, and shoulders
11. Drink a glass of water slowly
12. Light a candle or use essential oils (lavender, peppermint)

Mindful Moments

13. Guided meditation (Headspace, Insight Timer, YouTube)
14. Gratitude journalling (write down 3 things you're thankful for)
15. Body scan relaxation
16. Visualisation of a peaceful place
17. Prayer or quiet reflection
18. Colouring or doodling

Movement for Mood

19. Go for a short walk
20. Do 10 push-ups or squats to shift energy
21. Stretch your back and hips
22. Dance to one upbeat song
23. Gentle stretch poses

Joy Sparks

24. Call or message a friend who lifts you up
25. Listen to a favourite uplifting playlist
26. Watch a short funny video or comedy clip
27. Make a cup of tea/coffee and savour it without distractions
28. Hug someone (or even yourself!)
29. Play with a pet

Indulgent & Restorative Self-Care

30. Take a warm bath with Epsom salts or bubbles
31. Book a massage or spa treatment
32. Light candles and play relaxing music in your home
33. Have a nap without guilt
34. Enjoy a skincare ritual (face mask, moisturiser, exfoliation)
35. Treat yourself to a favourite meal or dessert
36. Spend time in nature (beach, forest, park)
37. Wake up early to have uninterrupted time for yourself (journalling, reading, exercise, or simply enjoying peace)
38. Curl up with a cosy blanket and a good book
39. Watch a favourite feel-good movie

Contribution & Kindness (Joy through Giving)

40. Write a thank-you card or message to someone
41. Donate clothes, food, or money to a cause you care about
42. Volunteer your time for a community group or charity
43. Cook a meal for a friend, neighbour, or family member
44. Pay for someone's coffee or meal anonymously
45. Offer to help a colleague with a task without being asked
46. Give genuine compliments throughout the day
47. Share your skills or knowledge to help someone grow
48. Mentor or encourage someone who's just starting out
49. Surprise someone with flowers, a treat, or a small gift

Creative Ideas

50. Read a few pages of a book you enjoy
51. Work on a creative hobby (painting, cooking, knitting)
52. Write down your thoughts to "empty your mind"

53. Declutter a small space (like your desk or bag)
54. Plan a fun activity for later in the week
55. Try a new recipe just for fun
56. Explore a local market, gallery, or event
57. Learn something new (a language, skill, or craft)
58. Rearrange or refresh a room in your home
59. Create a vision board for inspiration
60. Listen to a podcast or audio book that uplifts you

*(**Tip:** Select from the ideas above or create your own personal ones that you know will help you feel calm, joyful, or fulfilled.)*

FINAL THOUGHTS

You've now explored all four parts of the S3C Method: Self-Worth, Clarity, Consistency, and now, Calm. Together, they form the foundation of a more fulfilling life.

Because calm isn't a luxury. It's the power source behind everything you're trying to build. Start small. One breath. One prayer. One written gratitude at a time. That's how you anchor yourself through every season; growing stronger, not just striving harder.

In the next chapter, we'll bring everything together and give you clear, practical steps on what to do once you've finished reading this book, so you can move from insight to action and start living your own version of 360° success.

REFLECTION PROMPTS

1. What activities make me feel deeply calm and centred?
2. What are 3 things I am grateful for right now?
3. Where in my week can I create more space to just be?

Section 8. Conclusion – The Journey of 360° Success

"Success isn't what you build. It's who you become while building it."

When you first picked up this book, maybe you were feeling stuck. Maybe you were thriving in business but craving more balance.

Or maybe you simply knew, deep down, that you were made for a life of deeper peace, impact, and joy, not just endless achievement.

Now, you've taken the most important step: You've become aware. You've seen that success isn't just about numbers or accolades, it's about alignment across your whole life:

1. **Empowered Connection:** Friends, colleagues, business network, community, contribution

2. **Business Freedom:** Time and financial independence
3. **Self-Mastery:** Body, mind, and soul
4. **Family Balance:** Partner, kids, and extended family
5. **Life Experiences:** Adventure, travel, hobbies, joy

These are the pillars that create 360° Success, a life you don't need a holiday from.

A life where you wake up grateful, go to bed fulfilled, and live every day aligned with what truly matters.

But knowledge alone isn't enough.
Transformation happens through action.

THE TWO RULES OF HAPPINESS

Tony Robbins once said, *"Progress equals happiness."* And it's true, the feeling of fulfilment doesn't come from reaching a destination, but from knowing we're moving forward.

Yet most people lose that feeling of progress because they drift through life without direction, or they push so hard without ever pausing to appreciate how far they've come.

To stay in that beautiful state of progress, there are two simple rules to follow:

1. Intention

Be proactive. Design what you want. Don't wait for life to happen, decide how you want it to look. Set clear goals, create plans, and move with purpose. When you live with intention, you stop reacting and start directing your life. You become the architect of your days rather than a passenger.

2. Reflection

Take time to look back. Progress only feels real when you see it. Reflection allows you to measure, to take stock, to celebrate wins, and to learn from what didn't go as planned. This isn't about judgement, it's about awareness. Without reflection, life becomes a blur; with it, you build wisdom.

One key habit that has transformed my own life is building rhythms of reflection. I reflect daily, weekly, monthly, quarterly, and yearly. Each level serves a purpose, from small course corrections to big-picture perspective. It takes effort, yes, but it's worth every moment.

Because when you make reflection part of your lifestyle, you never lose sight of your progress. You stay grounded, grateful, and growing. Together, these two rules: Intention and Reflection, keep the wheel of growth turning. One drives you forward, the other grounds you. One gives direction, the other gives depth.

YOUR FIRST STEP: BUILD YOUR 30-DAY 360° PLAN

Big changes don't happen in a single leap. They happen through small, focused actions, repeated consistently over time.

Every chapter in this book included action steps; small, practical shifts you could implement straight away. Now is the time to revisit them and make sure you complete the exercises throughout the book.

To help you get started, I want to give you a simple 30-day practice that builds momentum without overwhelm.

Create a Kinder Morning

For the next 30 days, wake a little earlier and use that space for yourself. If early mornings feel hard, begin by rising 10 to 15 minutes earlier for the first week, then add 10 to 15 minutes each week until you reach the time that feels right for you.

What to do in that quiet pocket

1. **Arrive:** drink water and sit somewhere calm.
2. **Journal:** three short prompts
    1. What's currently on my mind?
    2. What are my top three impactful tasks today?
    3. What might get in the way, and how will I respond?
3. **Intend:** write one clear intention for how you want to show up.
4. **Centre:** prayer, gratitude, or stillness. One minute is enough to start.
5. **Review:** skim your highlights from this book. Circle one idea to apply today.
6. **Move:** 5 to 30 minutes of movement daily (e.g. walk, pilates, stretch, strength)

Mastering yourself is the foundation of 360° Success. When your mind, body, and soul are cared for and aligned, the other pillars become easier. You begin to think more clearly, choose more wisely, and act with steadier energy. That is why this practice comes first. After the first two weeks begin linking your mornings to the five pillars.

Choose one small action for each.

- **Empowered Connection:** connect with one new person per month
- **Business Freedom:** make one decision that simplifies your work.
- **Self Mastery:** read 10 pages of a personal development book per day
- **Family Balance:** say gratitudes with family every night before bed
- **Life Experiences:** schedule one micro joy for the week.

To keep measuring your growth, I encourage you to complete the quiz at **linhpodetti.com/quiz**. It will help you see clearly what is working well and what needs attention.

Keep revisiting your five pillars, notice where the gaps are, and commit to the tiniest steps you can take. Remember, it is those small actions, repeated consistently, that will transform your life.

REAL STORIES OF COURAGEOUS CHANGE

Let me leave you with a couple of real-life stories that show what's possible when you start living with intention.

Sharleen is a mother of two and a busy business owner. For years, she struggled to wake up early and constantly felt behind. But instead of giving up, she focussed on building the habit of waking up.

That one habit helped her build a consistent morning routine. Now, she has time to work out and focus on her new business before her kids even wake up. She feels more in control, energised, and at peace.

Jon, another entrepreneur, made the brave decision to quit alcohol. He realised that even though he wasn't drinking every day, it was still impacting his energy, mood, and mental clarity.

Since quitting, his life has become more stable, more joyful, and more aligned, not just in business, but in every area of his life.

These aren't just habits. They're daily choices that compound over time, building towards a life of true, sustainable success.

A SPECIAL THANKS

As I bring this book to a close, I want to honour a few key people whose encouragement helped bring this message to life. Their belief in me came at pivotal moments and their impact will forever be part of this journey.

Ray Esquieres, co-founder of Roll'd, one of Australia's most iconic Vietnamese street food franchises and EO Melbourne member. Thank you for seeing something in me and inviting me to deliver a workshop that gave me permission to lean into this passion. That workshop wasn't just a speaking gig, it was a defining moment.

Jacob Puthenparambil, my EO Singapore friend, thank you for encouraging me to pursue what became my "Linh's Life System" and even giving it its name. You saw the framework in my lived experience and nudged me to share it with the world.

Richard Evensen, my online mentor, your presence has been one of the most meaningful surprises on this journey. We've never met in person, but your encouragement from afar has deeply touched my heart. You first read my 40 Productivity Hacks book and then began following my posts about 360° Success. You became one of my most generous supporters offering detailed, thoughtful feedback and cheering me on with every step.

What's so striking and deeply moving is how much your life mirrored the 360° Success message. You had already stepped away from the hustle, retired young, travelled the world, and designed a life of joy, presence, and contribution.

You were living the very values this book stands for before I ever wrote them down.

And then came the unexpected: a brain tumour diagnosis at 59. In the midst of your best years, fit, happy, and thriving, you were faced with the unthinkable. Yet even now, as you walk through this incredibly hard season, you continue to lead with wisdom, humour, and a heart full of love.

You told me:

> *"You could call this book the Executive's Hack Bible... because these are the tools all of us need to succeed in every part of life."*

That meant so much to me. But even more powerful is the way you continue to embody that message, even now. Choosing gratitude over despair. Connection over isolation. Purpose over fear.

To everyone reading this: Please keep Richard in your prayers. Pray for healing. Pray for strength and peace for both him and his partner Heather. And let his story be a living reminder that the time to live fully is not one day, it's today.

Richard, you didn't just believe in this work, you lived it. And now, this book carries your fingerprints and your light.

To my incredible team at *Outsourcing Angel,* thank you for believing in this mission and supporting me not only as your founder, but as someone walking this journey beside you. Your dedication gave me the freedom to focus, write, and create from the heart. And to my friends and community members who've embraced the 360° Success framework as your own, thank you. Your stories, your feedback, your growth, they fuel this movement. Because of your belief, this book exists. You reminded me that my lived experience mattered. And I carry your encouragement with me always.

FINAL THOUGHTS

As we wrap up, I want to encourage you to pause and reflect: If you only had twelve months left to live, how would you live differently?

Whatever your answer is, let it guide your next step. You don't need to overhaul your whole life overnight, just take one small action each day toward a more fulfilled life. A life that goes beyond business wins and embraces joy, peace, and purpose.

Now is the time to stop waiting. Live a life of no regret. Step boldly into your version of 360° Success, starting today.

You've got this. And I'll be cheering you on every step of the way. I love to hear from you, email me your questions or suggestions to ***linh@outsourcingangel.com.au.*** You are never alone on this journey.

With love and belief in you,

Linh Podetti

Founder & CEO

Outsourcing Angel

www.outsourcingangel.com

"New outcomes require new actions, and the most important investment you'll make is in yourself."

- Linh Podetti

www.ingramcontent.com/pod-product-compliance
Lightning Source LLC
LaVergne TN
LVHW010600100826
845148LV00014B/2787

* 9 7 8 1 7 6 3 7 7 9 8 4 6 *